Education for Renewal

Books by David J. Ernsberger
Published by The Westminster Press®

Education for Renewal

A Philosophy of Adult Christian Education

Education for Renewal

by
DAVID J. ERNSBERGER

Philadelphia
THE WESTMINSTER PRESS

LIBRARY OF CONGRESS CATALOG CARD NO. 65-10578

PUBLISHED BY THE WESTMINSTER PRESS®
PHILADELPHIA, PENNSYLVANIA

PRINTED IN THE UNITED STATES OF AMERICA

To my wife Deborah

Contents

Preface

WHEN I was writing the last few pages of *A Philosophy of Adult Christian Education* back in 1958, a section that was concerned with Christian family life education and vocational study groups, I was touching on an aspect of adult education that has become increasingly prominent in my thinking and in my pastoral ministry: the education of the laity for their various forms of ministry in the world. Many writers, including myself, have warmly commended this aspect of adult education to the churches, but for the most part only in highly generalized and therefore rather unhelpful terms. Books on Christian education and on the laity keep referring to lay training for ministries in all realms of secular life, but tend to leave unanswered many basic questions as to how this kind of educational enterprise is to be carried on, the extent to which the local church or some other institutional forms of the Christian mission should undertake it, and some of the resources that are available. Compared with the rather massive amounts of guidance materials that have been written concerning general adult education in the content of the Christian message and concerning special adult education for leadership and service tasks within the local church, the subject of education for leadership and service in the world outside the church has been relatively untouched. In an effort to help fill the void, this book takes up the subject where I left it six years ago.

A number of resources and experiences that have come to me in the intervening years have contributed substantially to the development of the ideas expressed here. For two and a half years my former church in Michigan was one of thirteen churches whose clergy, together with representative lay leaders, were involved with the Institute for Advanced Pastoral Studies in suburban Bloomfield Hills and the nearby Detroit Industrial Mission and the Parishfield Community in a joint experimental project aimed at improving communication between clergy and laity concerning their respective tasks in fulfilling the church's mission in the world. Reports of experiments in parish renewal and other insights were shared at periodic meetings involving the staffs of the three sponsoring institutions in addition to the clergy and laity of the churches. I am considerably indebted to the creative thinking shared with me in the course of this experimental project, and in subsequent contacts, by Reuel Howe and Paul Nicely, of the Institute for Advanced Pastoral Studies, Francis O. Ayres, of Parishfield, and Robert C. Batchelder, Scott Paradise, and Hugh White, of Detroit Industrial Mission. In addition, it has been my good fortune during the past two years to be associated with Compton Allyn, executive director of the Cincinnati Industrial Mission, in a study group for clergy and in a discussion group of General Electric engineers and other technical personnel, drawn mostly from my congregation. Too numerous to mention are the other clergy, and the considerable numbers of lay people, from whom I have learned much of both theoretical and practical value in various experiments in my own church and elsewhere. I am also indebted to the lecture invitations that drew me to start writing on this subject of parish strategy and program for the nurture of lay Christian witness in secular life. This book developed out of four lectures delivered before the Synod of Toronto and Kingston of the Presbyterian Church of Canada, on October 16–17, 1962, and before an eastern area conference of Christian educators of the American Baptist Convention, January 15–16, 1963.

D.J.E.

Greenhills Community Church (Presbyterian)
Cincinnati, Ohio

Chapter I

Education for Institutionalism

THE PREDOMINANT and prevailing pattern of adult education in the church today is essentially irrelevant to the true mission of the church. The whole content of this first chapter is a series of footnotes to that proposition or, rather, that indictment. Perhaps it should be stated even more strongly. The education adults receive in their churches, in both formal and informal ways, can with good reason be accused of being even worse than irrelevant. A case can be made for the contention that it is not only irrelevant but that it is also in outright conflict with the Biblical understanding of the church's mission. It is in effect a contradiction of mission, a repudiation of mission.

This generalization is made with regard to the *pattern* of adult education in the church, not with regard to the *program* of adult education. A church's planned and structured program of adult education may make very deliberate and conscientious provision for the communication of Biblical affirmations concerning the mission of the church, and yet that same church's pattern of adult education—by which is meant all that adults learn through all their experiences in the church—may be a glaring refutation of such affirmations. The program consists of what most clergy and church officers consider to be the primarily educational functions of the church. The program, as such, usually touches only a minority of the adults, a fact that educators in the church regularly bewail. The pattern of adult education, as contrasted with the program, consists in the general style or flavor of congregational life, the general attitudes and assumptions that are communicated in one way or another to virtually everyone who comes into any sort of significant contact with the church. The program communicates certain meanings to that certain few who go out of their way to respond to it; the pattern communicates meanings, especially in nonverbal and symbolic ways, to just about everybody. The program you seek out; the pattern you soak up as part of the congregational atmosphere.

The pattern of adult education includes the program, and much more besides it. It is the pattern of adult education that is implied in the following definition of "curriculum" which has been rather widely accepted for many years: "the total organized provision made by the churches to guide and enrich the experience of those who take part in their activities." If we are to make meaningful evaluations of adult education in the church, we should keep in mind this more inclusive definition of it, or some similarly broad conception of its scope. What is communicated in nonprogrammed ways is often of far greater significance in determining the actual nature of the church, and people's ways of thinking about the church, than what is communicated through the more formal program of education. Therefore, if there is in fact a contradiction between program and pattern, between what is formally taught and what is actually and organizationally practiced concerning the mission of the church, then the actual practice is likely to outweigh the official theological line in determining what the church is really communicating to its people.

Lip Service Versus Self-serving Practice

In analyzing social organizations and institutions, sociologists frequently find it helpful to make a distinction between what may be called the *official* principles and the *working* principles that characterize them. The official principles or doctrines or positions of an organization or institution are openly treated with respect or even with reverence as definitions of its purpose. The working principles, on the other hand, are the actual operational standards and values by which the social system functions. The two sets of principles are seldom identical, and sometimes they are very far apart. For example, a given social system may have democratic procedure as part of its official principles, and yet one of its working principles may be that of functioning very autocratically. Similarly, it may officially espouse a principle of open membership while actually functioning according to a principle of exclusivism, or it may have a principle of service as its reason for existence while in fact its motivating principle could be primarily the self-centered satisfaction of gregarious impulses.

It is possible to examine the church itself in terms of such an analytical distinction; for whatever else the church may be or may be intended to be, it too is a social system with both official doctrines and working doctrines. And like most other social systems, there is a very considerable disparity between the two. Indeed, the official doctrines and the working doctrines of the church concerning its nature and mission are often poles apart. The gulf that separates them is not simply a matter of the actual inevitable falling short of the ideal. The disparity is not caused merely by human failure to actualize an ideal principle. The contradiction within the life of the church is more basic than that. For the working, functional doctrine by which the church actually lives is regarded by vast numbers of clergy and laymen alike, not as a regrettable though necessary compromise falling short of an official doctrine, but as a semiofficial doctrine in its own right. The official doctrine, the Biblical doctrine of the church's mission, frequently is not really understood or it is simply ignored. The working doctrine of the church's reality and mission, its pragmatic operational definition, is regarded by the majority of the laity and by a sizable number of the clergy as being normative and official. Those who take this position see essentially no contradiction or conflict between the official definition and the operational definition of the church's nature and purpose. Only those who have at least some rudimentary awareness of the normative Biblical view of the church see the contradiction. They alone perceive the hypocrisy of a church speaking simultaneously out of both sides of its mouth, saying one thing in its official statements and saying something quite different in the organization and emphases of its institutional life.

In contrast with official theological doctrine, the generally operative doctrine of the church defines it essentially as an institution, primarily concerned with its own institutional interests and statistical aggrandizement, uninterested in the world outside its structures except insofar as the world affects the institution. This is the understanding of the church which the church has been most effective in communicating to people. This is the message it has gotten across as the core of its *pattern* of adult education, whatever its formal *program* of adult education may have been. As a matter of fact, even the formal program has been very effective in conveying this anti-Biblical doctrine of the church's essential purpose. It has conveyed this spurious yet operational definition, not in so many words but, rather, by the general emphasis and direction of the formal parish education program considered as a whole. Whatever words are used, whatever pious protestations to the contrary may be made, the general impression created by the total educational offerings of the parish church is that this church is primarily concerned with its own maintenance and advancement. The program of adult education that the church provides is in large measure responsible for creating this impression. The overwhelming majority of the educational opportunities it offers are directly calculated to further the church's institutional interests above any other consideration.

This statement may seem unduly harsh and exaggerated until one pauses to analyze these educational offerings by the criterion of whether they primarily work for the institution's benefit or for the benefit of the world outside the institution, or at the very least for the benefit of the laity in living as Christians in that world. Admittedly, a very sizable portion of these educational offerings, namely, those which can be classed as general Bible study or doctrinal study, do not seem to fit into either category. Such general religious education furthers the church's institutional interests only in an indirect way, merely by increasing the kind of general religious knowledge that makes for more effective workers within the institution. By the same token, this generalized kind of adult enlightenment is of only indirect benefit to the world outside the church, and the life of the laity in that world. Often the world does not even benefit indirectly, because the orientation and general atmosphere of church life may have created the conviction that growing in religious knowledge is a worthy goal in and of itself.

When people take up a church's educational offerings as a sort of pious exercise, unrelated to the rest of life except perhaps by platitudinous, irrelevant, and moralistic generalizations offered in the learning situation, the impact is neither church-centered nor world-centered, but self-centered in the learner's smug feeling of having performed a work of merit merely by his participation. Like any other religious observance, theological reflection can become an idolatrous end in itself. Surely, laymen in the churches are as prone to this temptation as are seminarians. Theological conceptualization very easily becomes a substitute for, rather than an important discipline preliminary to, obedient action in the world. A concentrated program emphasis on greater Biblical and theological literacy among lay people does not lead them inevitably to a heightened awareness of or involvement in their secular ministries. In any event, the general program of Christian education, centering on Biblical or historical or doctrinal studies, serves neither the institutional church nor the layman's life outside the church in any direct way; and it is not likely to be of even much indirect assistance to the layman's secular life and witness if the general posture of the church, and therefore of its educational program, is preponderantly oriented inward toward the needs and concerns of the institution and away from the world in which God has placed it to serve.

The introverted posture that the church presents to people inside it as well as to those outside it through the kind of educational emphasis it makes is revealed most dramatically in its specialized, pragmatically oriented education program rather than in its program of general religious education. In almost every church, the preponderant emphasis in adult education is upon training classes to prepare people for various responsibilities within the church's institutional structure, an emphasis generally referred to in the jargon as "leadership education." It is interesting to note that this phrase, "leadership education," almost invariably refers to education for leadership within the institutional church, and almost never to training for Christian lay leadership in secular affairs.

Thus narrowly conceived, leadership education in the form of training for church school teaching, youth group advising, women's work leadership, annual financial canvassing, and other similar institutional jobs involves a far higher proportion of the church's total membership than does the program of general Christian education. And such church-job training outweighs the tiny remainder of the special educational program, such as parents discussion groups, specialized vocational study groups, and groups devoted to the study of social issues, by an even more overwhelming preponderance. Therefore, the formal educational experience of the great majority of adults in the church conveys to them the general impression that Christian education for adults principally amounts to training in how to perform various church jobs. Now, no one will dispute the necessity of the church's responsibility to train workers for its many institutional needs, but when such training receives such a preponderant emphasis at the same time that other forms of educational experience are being slighted, it is inevitable that the general impression created by the church's educational program in its entirety will be one that reinforces an image of the church's institutional self-centeredness.

This anti-Biblical conception of the church's purpose is communicated not only by the way the church bulletin or calendar of educational activities strikes the eye, with church-job training having such overweening prominence, but also by the content of some of the educational-promotional emphases that are aimed at the church's entire constituency. The typical program of stewardship education is a case in point. The materials for stewardship education that descend from the denominational boards in a continuous deluge upon the churches have little if anything in their content that would suggest to people that their church has any other central concerns besides the expansion of its total membership and program budget. Where in all this mass of materials is there any suggestion that money expended upon objects other than the institutional church might also conceivably be glorifying God in other ways? What has this material to offer besides silence with regard to Christian attitudes toward donations to political parties, to united community funds, to colleges and universities, and to other significant charities? Or what has this material to say by way of guidance with regard to that majority of a family's income which is not given to any charitable cause, that majority which a family actually spends? The silence of these stewardship education materials on this subject seems to suggest that the church has nothing helpful to say to people in their role as consumers. It implies that stewardship is not to be understood as obedience to God in all aspects of economic expenditure, that stewardship involves only that portion which is given to the church, and that as far as the teachings of the church are concerned the remainder can be spent without any regard to the doctrine of God's sovereignty.

The silence of these stewardship promotional materials with regard to voluntary gifts to nonecclesiastical causes involves a failure to affirm political parties, colleges, and various humanitarian agencies in society as vital concerns of Christian citizenship. It implies that we are "giving to God" when we give our financial support to the church, but not when we give it to a political party. It implies that God is almost exclusively interested in the church, and that he has very little interest in political affairs, in questions of social and economic justice, in world peace, in the entire arena of man's social existence. It implies that giving food to the hungry and drink to the thirsty, welcoming the stranger and clothing the naked, are done as unto Christ only when they are done through ecclesiastical channels. To put it more bluntly, it conveys the impression that the church is downright greedy and jealous in an exceedingly self-centered way of any humanitarian, political, or educational institutions that are competitors for its members' dollars.

It is probably unfair to castigate those denominational officials who produce these stewardship promotion materials for neglecting the wider dimensions of education for Christian stewardship. They are merely doing the job assigned them by the denominations, namely, the promotion of giving to support the institutional needs both of the individual churches and of the denominations they comprise. The proper objects of blame are probably the clergy and the lay officers of the local churches, who generally fail to supplement these materials with a broader vision of what Christian financial responsibility implies beyond the claims and needs of the church. Occasionally, one hears of local stewardship education programs that present such praiseworthy ideas as the "modern tithe," recommending some portion of one's total proportionate giving to be designated for some of the various nonecclesiastical causes that also serve God's purposes in his world. But for the most part, the local program simply apes and echoes the ecclesiastical chauvinism of the denomination's mass promotion.

In all fairness, it must be admitted that the stewardship education program of the local church, while remaining largely silent concerning giving to nonecclesiastical causes, very often is broadened to include stewardship of "time and talents." Churches often include enlistment for various church responsibilities as part of their emphasis at the time of the general financial canvass. This certainly conveys a more inclusive and adequate conception of Christian stewardship. Yet it scarcely needs to be pointed out that while this emphasis is superior in that it solicits a more total commitment, it is just as faulty as the other in its introverted church-centeredness. It simply reinforces the image of the church as the only place where conscientious stewardship of time and abilities has any meaning, because it fails to affirm forms of community service that lie outside the church's institutional structures. Admittedly, much of the civic and social busywork in which the church's members are involved is utterly trivial and does not serve such redemptive purposes as, for example, helping to build authentic community within modern society; but this is hardly true of their involvement in a good many of their political and humanitarian organizations. The failure of the church's stewardship education program to lend affirmative support to such significant secular involvements strengthens the operative doctrine of the church as just one more voluntary association making demands and claims on people's time and energies—demands that are singularly unsympathetic to the claims of any other human association, regardless of its worth. Thus the general impression created by stewardship education on the minds of the people is one that reinforces the institution-centered doctrine of the church's mission and purpose.

The same is largely true of the mission education program of the church. This is sometimes called "missionary education," which is a more accurate title for it, since mission education tends to be simply education about missionaries and their doings. The activities of professional missionaries form the major themes of mission-study texts, family nights, and various local schools of missions programs. It helps to quell a congregation's inveterate tendency to be concerned only with its own local needs, and serves as a stimulus to the support of benevolent causes. However, the almost single-minded preoccupation of missionary education with missionaries and missions always somewhere else obscures the fact that the local church too *is* mission, and that each individual member also has a unique and crucial mission of his own where he lives and works and plays. Women's groups spend endless hours studying about someone else's mission halfway around the world, but hardly any time considering what their own mission is as wives and mothers, as consumers and citizens. Many of them seem to be escaping from a sense of boredom and meaninglessness and frustration in their own domestic and civic roles by vicarious participation in some missionary's mission. If half the program effort currently expended in studying somebody else's mission were devoted to helping create in people an awareness of their own specific mission where they are, the concept of the church as a missionary people, a fellowship existing for the sake of mission, would begin to dislodge the present popular concept of the church as simply an institution that *has* missions in various places and supports them.

A Dismaying Consensus of Clergy and Laity

It would be difficult to overestimate the extent to which the institution-oriented definition of the church's nature and mission is firmly implanted in the attitudes and expectations of both clergy and laity. The frequency with which clergy still refer to church vocations as "full-time

Christian service" illustrates the tenacity of this point of view. The clear implication of this time-worn epithet is that "Christian service" means only service to the ecclesiastical establishment, and that the best a Christian lay person has to offer is part-time Christian service through various forms of ecclesiastical housekeeping and odd jobs. Another indication of this widespread clerical attitude is to be seen in the gloating and genteel boasting many clergy indulge in when one of the sheep in their flock one day walks out of his place of employment and prepares to don the shepherd's mantle. Such men are often held up before the rest of the church as if their new calling were necessarily a "higher calling" for them. In many situations this may indeed be the case, but in others it may represent a flight from vocational responsibility in the world because the church has not helped the man to discover Christian meaning and opportunity in his secular employment. Placing these men on pedestals before the congregation as trophies won by the clergy only deepens the layman's feeling that his lifework, if it has any Christian meaning at all, is definitely of an inferior order.

Statistical confirmation of the clergyman's tendency to define the church essentially in institutional terms is given by the nationwide survey of Presbyterian families and clergymen conducted a few years ago by the Office of Family Education Research of The United Presbyterian Church in the U.S.A. A thousand Presbyterian clergymen gave written answers to the question: What does the church expect of Christian families? Fifty-six percent of the clergy gave answers that stressed family participation within the institutional structures of the church. They defined this as support of the church program both financially and personally, assisting in the educational program of the church, maintaining enthusiastic backing for the institution on the part of the family, and being present at public meetings and services of the parish. Only a minority of the clergy polled, a mere 31 percent, placed qualities of faith within family life ahead of institutional loyalty to the church. This minority of the clergy had stressed such virtues as loyalty to Christ, commitment to Christian witness, an understanding of missionary outreach, a vital prayer life, growth in faith, and personal commitment to the task of evangelism.

In their summary, the researchers declared: "It can fairly be concluded from these data that the average pastor tends overmuch to interpret his church life in subjective terms of its organization and only secondarily, and sometimes seldom, as commitment and witness to its Christian faith in home and community."[1] Gerhard Lenski, a sociologist at the University of Michigan, supports this conclusion with data drawn from a carefully designed sample of metropolitan Detroit's population, which was studied to determine the correlations between religious affiliation and economic and political values and behavior. Lenski discovered that a surprisingly high percentage of Detroiters were willing to have their clergy express themselves more freely on controversial issues. However, the clergy actually tended to engage in controversy to a far lesser extent than this, largely because of their institutional preoccupations. "The majority of the clergy of all faiths," Lenski concludes, "seem to be vigorous, hard-working men, skilled in what they take to be their major task: that of building their own parish or congregation."[2]

The responses of parents in the Presbyterian family life survey indicate that institution-obsessed clergymen have been immensely successful in "educating" their adults in this unofficial, operational doctrine of the church. In both questionnaires and interviews the parents indicated that purely institutional views of the church's reality prevailed among them. The summary of the research states that "remarks recorded from the interviews leave us with the strong impression that for these people the church means a bundle of organizations, a mass of activities, and a crew of willing volunteer workers (well, some less willing than others) who are engaged in about the same basic business as 'other character-building agencies.'"[3] The researchers go on to comment: "When institutional aspects of church life prevail in the thinking of the people, there is bound to be greater concern about keeping the wheels turning. As a result, parents sometimes complain about being loaded with too much responsibility. They speak of being caught in a veritable beehive of activity, all aimed at nurturing the organization rather than ministering to the world."[4] Thus, the church has allowed itself to be viewed by its people as an end in itself rather than as a means to an end. It frequently appears to them to be just one more organization that it is good for certain vague reasons for a community to have, an organization to be supported and nourished, although they are hard to put to describe the ways in which it nourishes *them* in their family life or in other dimensions of their daily existence.

A further illustration of this ingrained attitude among lay people is given in the experience of the staff of the Detroit Industrial Mission. The purpose of the Mission is to establish meaningful two-way communication between the church and the business and industrial community, to help men and women discover and actualize their Christian ministry in their vocational life. A large share of the staff's time is spent in seeing men in their offices, in union halls, at lunch or dinner, in their homes, and at management and union meetings. When a staff member makes his first contact, he finds that his man is often very suspicious. He expects that the staff member is visiting him in order to obtain some financial contribution or to enlist him for some chore in a local parish. Very often toward the end of the first visit he will say, "What is it that you really want?" When he discovers that the real interest of the Detroit Industrial Mission is in him and his job, the man is usually surprised and shocked. His parish experience has "educated" him to expect the church to be interested in and concerned about him only in certain aspects of his life away from his work, especially the enlistment of his time and ability for specific church duties.

Two of the cooperating clergymen in the Ecumenical Centre in Wilton, Connecticut, assert the prevalence of the same sort of expectations among the unchurched. The experience of almost all the vocational concern groups connected with the Centre has included, at least in the early stages, a rather wary and suspicious searching on the part of those unaffiliated with any of the churches for ecclesiastical attempts to "use" or manipulate them. They find it difficult to accept the fact that the purpose of the Centre is primarily an effort on the part of the sponsoring churches to serve and help them in their particular occupations, and not some covert strategy that is designed to gain more members or contribute to bigger church budgets. Herman G. Steumpfle encountered similar expectations with regard to the institutional church as he was assembling a group of public relations people for an experimental vocational ethics group in New York City: "There is genuine therapy," he writes, "in seeing ourselves as others see us—once we recover from the shock. Even in initial telephone contacts it was disconcerting to have the voice at the other end sometimes respond to the word 'church' with a recital of volunteer work already being done for religious and charitable groups. There was a conditioned reflex which identified an approach from the church as the prelude to a request for free professional services!"[5]

In the face of all the evidence, it is impossible to escape the dismaying conclusion that the churches have been unfortunately successful in educating adults in a distorted understanding of the mission of the church.

Chapter II

Education for Clericalism

THE DEMONSTRATED predominance of essentially institution-centered definitions of the reality and mission of the church in the thinking of both clergy and laity leads naturally to a consideration of two corollary definitions of the role of the laity within such an understanding of the church. These derivative corollaries concerning the laity are equally as anti-Biblical and prevalent as the operative conception of the church itself. The first of these two popular corollaries may be stated briefly as follows: *The primary locus for the ministry of the laity is not out in the world of the common life, but within the institutional framework of the church as an auxiliary ministry to the ministry of the clergy.* There is a widespread consensus among both clergy and laity that the chief mission of the laity is to be unsalaried assistants to the pastors of the churches. Thus the work of the church becomes narrowly defined as "church work." Statistical evidence for the prevalence of such a consensus among laymen is contained in the results of a recent survey of what Methodist laymen believe, conducted by a research group of faculty members from Boston University School of Theology. A questionnaire, administered to a very large representative sampling of the entire denomination, covered a wide range of matters concerning the Christian faith and its application to life. One of its categories was designed to test how laymen think of themselves. Respondents were asked to check which of the following definitions of the laity most nearly corresponded to their own personal views: (1) members of the people of God called to a total ministry of witness and service in the world; (2) those who are ministered to by the clergy who are the true church; (3) people in part-time Christian service; or (4) nonordained Christians whose function is to help the clergy. Out of over five thousand replies, an overwhelming 59.9 percent selected the fourth choice, defining the laity as assistants of the clergy.[6]

In his book *A Theology of the Laity* (The Westminster Press, 1959), Hendrik Kraemer analyzes American church life and charges that our concern with the laity has been chiefly expressed in attempts to get laymen more involved in institutional responsibilities in the local church. He speaks of the end products of these educational and promotional efforts to round up "more and more manpower" as "clericalized laymen" or "camouflaged ecclesiastics," men and women who generally are conscious of performing a ministry only when they are directly involved in those institutional activities we commonly refer to as church work. The educational pattern of the church has largely failed to communicate to these lay people an awareness that many of their functions outside the church are to be conceived of as ministries, as part of the work of the church, fully as much if not even more than their "church work." This educational failure of the church can rightfully be blamed in large measure on the clergy. Clergymen often show a singular lack of understanding of the nature and meaning of the work that their laymen are doing in the world, and they consistently fail to affirm it as the point at which the church as the people of God fulfills its divinely intended servant role to the world. Because clergymen so frequently fail to see many of the secular responsibilities of their people as an essential part of the task of the church, they cannot very well help their people to recognize them as such, with the result that both clergy and laymen tend to regard as church work only the services rendered to the church organization.

A good illustration of this clerical mind-set is given in the usage frequently accorded the phrase "the ministry of the laity." This phrase has emerged into great prominence in recent years, beginning with the Evanston Assembly of the World Council of Churches in 1954. The original emphasis in the use of the phrase, especially in ecumenical circles, was on the ministry of the laity *in the world.* However, it is presently used in many quarters simply as another slogan for institutional activism within the church. An example of this narrowed usage is to be found in Robert Raines's book, *New Life in the Church.* Early in his book, Raines lists as one sign of the loss of mission in the local church its overconcern with its own institutional life. But just a few chapters later, he lists some of the results of an emphasis on small study and prayer groups in his Cleveland church in a chapter titled "New Creation in the Church: The Lay Ministry Emerges." He points out just what he means by this "lay ministry." "First," he writes, "the lay ministers are becoming leaders in the church." He then lists the many church positions and jobs that are being taken care of by people from these small groups. "Secondly," he says, "the lay ministers are operating as leaven in the church"; and he cites examples that are strictly within the framework of the church's institutional life. "Third, the lay ministers are accepting the call to preach," and he mentions how frequently his lay people take over the Sunday preaching responsibilities. "Fourth," he writes, "the lay ministers are training others for their ministry," by which he means that laymen have a large part in conducting the membership training classes for both youth and adults.[7]

New Life in the Church is a superb account of the emergence of that portion of lay ministry which is discharged within the institutional framework of the church. But like many other accounts of local renewal that are being so enthusiastically received today, the emphasis is on new life *within* the church rather than on new life *from* the church into *God's world,* with an attendant narrowing of the fullness of what is Biblically implied when we speak of the ministry of the laity.

Some of these local ventures in parish renewal are guilty not only of an unscriptural narrowing of what is meant by the ministry of the laity; they also distort its meaning by confusing the roles of clergy and laity. The pulpit ministry, and other ministries of public verbal proclamation, do not constitute the calling of each and every Christian. To be sure, many laymen do have charismatic gifts for public proclamation and an attendant conviction of being called to such a form of witness; but that is indeed far from saying that all laymen can or should make their witness in this manner. Yet many church leaders communicate the impression that the ministry of the laity will be fulfilled in direct proportion to the number of laymen we have playing at preaching through a multiplication of "Laymen's Sundays"; at any rate, they seem to imply that formal public proclamation is the noblest and most preferable vehicle for lay witness. Such a diffusion of the clerical role, whatever its debatable theological or pragmatic merits, burdens the laity with an essentially clerical definition of their role that tends to obscure the dimensions of their Christian calling, which transcend ecclesiastical structures.

The church must face up to the fact that the general run of activities in most parishes, including their educational activities, tend to divert people from, rather than to prepare them for, their various ministries in the world. As the devoted layman's work for the institution increases, his interest in and time for the world decreases. As an illustration of this, it is noteworthy that Gerhard Lenski, in his important study of the relationships between religious affiliation and social attitudes in metropolitan Detroit, found no evidence that greater institutional involvement in the churches accompanied the holding of more positive attitudes toward daily work and its meaning, despite the fact that the traditional Protestant emphasis on the doctrine of Christian vocation in daily work would lead us to expect some positive statistical correlation. On the contrary, it was found that those who were rather marginal in their relationship to the churches actually seemed a bit more likely to hold positive attitudes toward their work than those who were more institutionally active.[8]

It is usually those lay men and women who have the fullest Christian maturity and commitment, together with the strongest motivations and greatest abilities for serving Jesus Christ in political, civic, and vocational life, who are often busiest with church activities. The recruitment of leadership in the local congregation usually follows the line of least resistance, following the old adage that if you want a job done, ask a busy man. The preoccupation of these leaders with responsibilities within the congregational structure not only draws them away from opportunities for ministry outside the church but also keeps them too busy to be on the receiving end of educational opportunities provided by the church which might help equip them for these secular ministries. Those devoted lay people who are on school boards or active in their political party or community chest appeal, or in business or trade associations, often feel guilty because they "aren't doing more for the church," as they say. They are made to feel guilty because the church seldom communicates to them any affirmative support with regard to these outside functions. Therefore, they conceive of these responsibilities as being in conflict with, rather than as complementary to, their involvement within the church. Their sense of guilt is in direct proportion to their sense of loyalty to the institutional aspects of the church.

The report of the study section on the laity given at the Evanston Assembly of the World Council of Churches stressed the importance of freeing more lay leaders from hobbling, confining commitments to the institutional structures of the church. It stated: "Many laymen must be rescued from the isolating realm of mere church busyness, in order that they may serve Christ where they earn and spend their money. . . . The real battles of the faith today are being fought in factories, shops, offices, and farms, in political parties and government agencies, in countless homes, in the press, radio and television, in the relationship of nations." But heedless of the wisdom of this statement, business proceeds as usual in the typical church on the corner. The creative thought and energies of the most mature and deeply committed people continue to be almost exclusively preempted and consumed in the mere maintenance of the church as an institution. If the church's educational program does include any features that would help prepare these people for their ministry as parents, consumers, citizens, and workers, they are kept too busy leading to find time to be led by them. Like Martha, so busy serving the Lord that she felt she could not spare the time to be served by the Lord by learning at his feet with Mary, these conscientious laymen are so preoccupied with ministering to the needs of the church that they can scarcely pause to be ministered unto for the sake of their ministry to the world.

A second popular corollary concerning the life of the laity is really a negative form of the first corollary, which maintains that the ministry of the laity is merely an auxiliary ministry within the church. According to this second corollary, *the world of daily work has no intrinsic connection with the work of the church*. The staff of the Detroit Industrial Mission reports that the most frequent response with which they meet, as much from church members as from those outside the church, is that there is no significant relationship between the Christian faith and what they are doing and facing in their work. The recorded remarks of a draftsman interviewed in one of the large automobile plants in Detroit are illustrative of this pervasive frame of mind: "Well, yes, I think a lot about Christianity. After all, I'm on the church board and of course we go to church on Sunday. But weekdays when I'm at work—I'm a draftsman—well, I don't see any connection. What's Christianity got to do with a drafting board? I can see no Christian significance in my work at all. God is concerned with relationships and the only time I do something with Christian bearing in my job is when I drink coffee and talk with my fellow draftsmen at the office, and then I'm not at work, but 'goofing off.' Just tell me what I can do in a job like that."

Doubtless that draftsman speaks for a very large proportion of lay people. The realm of work seems to many of them to be beyond the scope of God's redemptive activity. For a sizable portion of them, work remains what it appears to be in the third chapter of Genesis after Adam's fall. Work is a curse, a necessary evil to be endured: eight hours endured simply for the sake of the other sixteen, five days of the week endured simply for the sake of the weekend. And even in those cases where work is satisfying or meaningful or even exciting to the lay people, these affirmative aspects of work are seldom perceived as being related to Christian affirmations concerning work's meaning. One of the reasons for this is that usually today the place where a man works is separated from the place where he lives. He is a commuter between a business area and a residential area, between a sphere of production and a sphere of consumption, where his family lives. The separation is not only geographical, but also psychological and spiritual.

Furthermore, the separatism between these two spheres is ethical; and the educational program of the churches has had perhaps its most conspicuous failure with regard to this ethical dimension. Laymen seem to have received little help from their churches in facing the ethical ambiguities of their occupations. Their "Christian education" has consisted of moralistic generalizations that take no real cognizance of these ambiguities. Confronted by their churches with a legalistic interpretation of what it means to be a Christian in one's vocational life, their sense of a cleavage between faith and work becomes even more deeply ingrained in their self-awareness. Seldom does one encounter a layman with any understanding of what the gospel message of justification by faith might imply with regard to some of the utterly irreconcilable conflicts between the demands of Christian ethical norms and the intrinsic demands of the job situation. The conviction that God is both served and met, in mercy as well as in judgment, at every point of decision and responsibility in our lives in a fallen world, seldom seems to have been brought home to them.

Because of the tremendous cleavage between sacred and secular in the minds of most lay people as they regard their daily work, and perhaps to help compensate for their unresolved sense of guilt concerning ethical dilemmas connected with their work, many of them look at work in the institutional activities of the church as a haven of Christian meaning or as a place for performing compensatory good works that will atone for their failures to meet absolute ethical norms in their occupations. In his book *The Suburban Captivity of the Churches,* Gibson Winter suggests the significant role a sense of guilt may play in the performance of ecclesiastical duties. He refers to the frantic organizational overactivity of the "organization church" as a "Protestant penitential system," in which the pastor performs, at least unconsciously, the priestly role of easing guilty lay consciences as he assigns institutional tasks that actually amount to a form of legalistic penance. This may be a rather overdrawn caricature of the place of guilt in the hyperactivism of the organization church. But there is no question that the church is an isolated oasis of Christian meaning, if it is not a place for performing penance, in the minds of many.

Very often people find the deepest expression of the gospel in the relationships they experience within the fellowship of the local church. Such people do not find the same satisfactions and significance on the job or in their homelife; but they learn to live with it, to endure it, to get along with it somehow, aided and sustained by the satisfying experiences they have among friends in their parish activities. In a sense, the parish becomes for them a refuge and an escape from their meaningless and unsatisfying life at work or at home. Obviously, this kind of recourse to the church is not in itself reprehensible. Surely the institutional church has a ministry of healing within its own life to men and women in their brokenness, their loneliness and emptiness. But if the church unreflectively does nothing more than aid them in their running away from secular life, without helping them to perceive potential meaning and satisfaction in it, then it is only widening that pernicious rift between life in the church and life in the world which robs them of a sense of wholeness.

Thus through all its avenues for communicating meanings, the general pattern of church life seems to have been eminently successful in communicating a partial and thereby distorted conception not only of what the church is, but also an equally distorted conception of the layman's role. These distortions have been "taught" so successfully and thoroughly that no formal catechizing is needed. But if these distorted meanings were to be cast in catechetical form, they might read as follows:

QUESTION 1. What is the church? ANSWER: The church is an institution, made up of an intricate complex of subsidiary organizations, most of whose functions take place in a church building.

QUESTION 2. What is its purpose? ANSWER: The purpose of the church is to grow and expand, absorbing more and more people, and more and more of their time and money, within its structures.

QUESTION 3. What is the main responsibility of its laymen? ANSWER: Their main responsibility is to assist the ministers in carrying out the church's institutional purposes.

This is the partial, truncated vision of the church most devoutly held among us. This is the heresy which, operationally at least, has become orthodoxy.

This unofficial, functional description of the nature and purpose of the church presently so dominates the thoughts and actions of both clergy and laity that, at the risk of elaborating the obvious, we need to remind ourselves of the classical Christian conception of the church in its fullness. To be sure, definitions of the church that stress its institutional embodiment are indeed partially valid because certain institutional forms are essential to the church's existence. Institutional self-preservation and maintenance are legitimate functions of the church because of the very fact of our collective humanity and its concrete institutional requirements. The church as the people of God must be nourished in its gathered life within the institution so that it may be prepared to do its work in its dispersed life. But the church's institutional occupations and concerns are properly only necessary means to an end, namely, its mission of witness and service in and to the world outside it.

The church must live by and for its mission to the world, for it was "the world" that God so loved that he sent his only-begotten Son to redeem it. The church, as Dietrich Bonhoeffer has reminded us, is mission. It is the company of the elect, the chosen, God's people in the world, in exodus from the realm of religious isolation. Yet as God's people in the world, the church does not exist for the purpose of manipulating or dominating the world. Paul's reference to the church as a "colony of heaven" (Phil. 3:20, Moffatt translation) is homiletically popular, but the word "colony" carries an unfortunate connotation of institutional empire-building. But though the church's proper relation to the world is not one of trying to swallow the world up in its institutional imperium, neither is it the church's function merely to exist as a totally insulated and segmented aspect of it. The church's task in relation to the world is, as Bishop Wickham has said, to understand it, to prophesy within it, and to stain it.[9] This is the church's true "worldliness," its existence in and for the world.

The message that the church has been commissioned to teach is a message about the world, a declaration that God was in Christ reconciling the world unto himself. The church, which exists in the world, is also sent into the world. It is called to become ever more deeply committed as both apostle and servant to the world, because in Christ, God has committed himself without reservation to the overcoming of the world's estrangement from him. The otherworldliness of the church, especially as manifested in its self-preoccupation, does not harmonize with the worldliness of God, who created the world, who spoke and acted through its history, and who in the fullness of time entered it in the incarnation. We act as Christians when we do what Christ did in the world, which was not only to proclaim the good news of what God is doing in history, but also to exercise care of and responsibility for others in the world.

This conception of the church's mission implies an understanding of the ministry of the laity as having two points of focus, the needs of the world outside the church as well as the institutional needs of the church itself. Arnold Come in *Agents of Reconciliation* demonstrates that *diakonia,* the New Testament word for "service" or "ministry," had world-centered as well as church-centered connotations. The church-centered connotation predominates in the New Testament, he maintains, simply because in its beginning stages the early church obviously had to concentrate on its own establishment. But even from the earliest period, it was understood that the ultimate purpose of mutual ministry to one another within the church was as preparation for various ministries in the people's daily dispersion in the common life.[10]

An idea of what this conception of the mission of the church and of the ministry of its laity implies for the ordering of church life is suggested in a statement commended by the Central Committee of the World Council of Churches: "When the Church is assembled, it is then a token of the Communion of Saints, rendering praise and intercession to God on behalf of the world. Yet when the life of the Church is brought under the judgment of God's Word, we have to recognize that this judgment must fall on its *whole* life—scattered as well as assembled. One test of the life of the Church in its assembled aspect—in worship, church government and organizations—is how this part of its life contributes to the life of the scattered Church. Thus it is the task of the pastor and other professional church workers not only to be concerned with the assembled Church, but to prepare the laity for their distinctive ministry." Actually, this seems to be the conception in the mind of Paul when he speaks of Christ's gifts as including some men given to the church as "pastors and teachers, to equip God's people for work in his service" (Eph. 4:12, *The New English Bible*).

If the clergy are to fulfill this kind of ministry *to* the laity for the sake of strengthening the distinctive ministry *of* the laity, it would seem that there must be far more conversation between clergy and laity concerning their respective ministries than presently exists. The life of the church today suffers from a lack of communication, and therefore a lack of understanding, between clergy and laity on these matters. We noted in the previous chapter that lay people have a reasonably accurate picture of their proper role within the structures of the church. They accurately perceive that the chief minister in the gathered church, with its focus on worship, pastoral, educational, and organizational functions, is the pastor, with the lay members serving as his assistants. There is a fairly well established consensus of clergy and laity concerning their respective roles within church structures. However, both clergy and laity seem to misunderstand their own and each other's respective roles in the world outside the church. It does not seem to be generally understood that out in the world the roles of clergy and laity are properly reversed: that the chief minister of the church when it is dispersed and at work in the world is the layman, and that there the clergyman is *his* assistant and resource.

One illustration of this lack of understanding of who is called to do what in the world is the infrequency with which lay people turn to their clergymen for pastoral counseling involving job problems or civic concerns rather than just with their purely domestic and private problems. Perhaps this reticence on the part of laymen to discuss such "worldly" problems with their pastors is partly attributable to a widely held conviction that clergymen simply are not sufficiently knowledgeable concerning the world outside the church to be of much help in such matters. However, it would also seem to reflect a general conviction that pastors are rather unconcerned with counseling problems outside the scope of family relationships. But whatever may be the proximate causes of this general lay reticence, it is evident that as long as lay people are not led to perceive their responsibilities in the world as their ministry they are not likely to think of their pastor as their "assistant minister" in these secular involvements.

The clergyman's own failure to understand that he is called to minister in the world outside the church in an essentially secondary, auxiliary capacity beside his lay people is to be seen in the role he frequently assumes in Christian social action. Whether it's an attempt to close down a bar or open up a racially segregated neighborhood, or any other form of social action, clergymen often seem to dominate the operation. There is a general tendency to measure the social relevance and impact of the local church merely by the social witness of its minister, especially in his preaching. To listen to such preaching can be and often is helpful to those in the pew; but such preaching by itself, without any consequent wrestling with the issues in discussions among the lay members within the church, can also be a means of escape from a probing and vigorous application of the Christian message to the layman's own vocational and civic responsibilities. The relative ineffectiveness of such preaching in and of itself is indirectly indicated in this significant sociological finding that came out of the studies of the Detroit metropolitan area, as reported by Gerhard Lenski: that among white Protestants, the proportion of those who could properly be labeled as political and economic conservatives varied *directly* with the degree of involvement and participation in the life of their churches.[11]

Now it would be absurd to argue from this that associational involvement in white Protestant churches tends to make people more conservative. Obviously, other causal factors predominate in creating a conservative mentality. Still, inasmuch as the social pronouncements of the major Protestant denominations are anything but conservative by Lenski's survey criteria, and assuming that at least some of the pastors of these Detroit area churches conveyed the contents of some of their denominational pronouncements to their people through their preaching or perhaps through the printed word, the findings serve to give some substantiation to the assertion that preaching and other monological means of communication, forming as they do the major means of communication in most churches today, are relatively ineffective in changing people's attitudes and opinions on social questions.

Ringing social pronouncements coming from distant delegated assemblies of the denomination, and prophetic preaching, are relevant to the social ministry of the entire church only when they serve as a stimulus leading to creative dialogue among laymen seeking in a disciplined manner to determine the mind of Christ on the great questions of the day. Only by means of creating more opportunities for significant dialogue between clergy and laity can we hope to achieve any narrowing of the vast gulf that separates the social convictions of clergy and laity, the enormous disparity between the national pronouncements of the denominations (drafted, for the most part, by clergy and by rather thoroughly clericalized laymen) and the social attitudes of the average churchgoer.

The prophetic pastor who attempts to "go it alone" on social issues, who is too impatient to make any serious attempt to bring at least a portion of his people along with him through the educational program of the church, falls right into the trap of clericalism. He has usurped his people's rightful role as the chief ministers of the church in its social impact on the world by assuming that role himself. He has failed to enlist in God's service their superior gifts for this dimension of ministry, gifts based in considerable measure on their greater secular knowledgeability and their more effective influence on community power structures and decision-making elites. Indeed, the knowledgeability of lay leaders concerning the multitudinous facts of human social existence is so infinitely greater than the clergyman's that it is absurd for him to think he either should or can devise a detailed moral theology that he will then "teach" to his laymen, ready-made for them.

It is far more feasible to conceive of laymen learning enough theology so as to be able to think through and articulate a Christian social ethic for a given situation than it is to try to picture clergymen learning enough about the world to do the same. But neither of these alternatives is as sensible as that of relying on a continuing dialogue between clergy and laity which would employ to the fullest advantage the relative expertness of each in forging a viable Christian consensus on important social issues. In our present world, the issues of political, social, economic, and cultural policy have reached such a level of bewildering complexity that direct unilateral intervention by clergymen alone often results in statements or actions that are ludicrous in their oversimplification of the issues. Certainly, the church must speak and act in the world with regard to social issues. This is part of its prophetic ministry to the world, whether the world wants that ministry or not. But such prophetic speaking and acting is primarily the office of that majority of the church we call the laity, rather than of the professional clerical minority whose amateurish social witness presently is the predominant one.

It is almost equally true in rural or suburban or urban areas that problems of planning allocation of community resources for health, education, and welfare, and evaluation of needs for economic development, pose issues that require a very considerable degree of worldly competence and training, so much as to preclude the assumption that the clergyman is normally the most appropriate and qualified spokesman for the church on such questions. To utilize in the best manner the gifts and capabilities that have been variously distributed among God's people, both clergy and laity need to realize that the present prevalent pattern of clerical dominance and lay passivity in the area of social witness ought to be almost exactly reversed.

Thus the clergyman's conception of his proper role seems to be in need of correction and modification as much as does the layman's. Both have a fairly clear and Biblical conception of their respective functions within church structures. It is in respect to their ministries in the world outside the church that the greatest amount of misunderstanding exists. Therefore, the recovery of the full Biblical sense of mission would seem to require for its achievement a continuing dialogue between clergy and groups of laity about who they are and what they are called to be in the world. Each needs the help of the other in discovering their respective God-given identities.

In his contribution to the symposium, *Making the Ministry Relevant,* Reuel Howe gives us a vision of what such mutual teaching through dialogue could mean for the church:

> To reach men significantly with the Gospel in our times we must increase the ministry a hundredfold, and the only way of doing that is to return to the great Biblical doctrine of the priesthood of all believers and affirm again that all Christian men and women are servants and ministers of Christ and His Church. If the whole ministry of the Church were to be activated for the Church's mission to the world, the role of the clergy would have to be different. The major part of his responsibility would be to train and direct the work of the laymen as they witness to Christ in that part of the world in which they live.[12]

That is a noble vision of the church. It is also a very large order—unattainably large, some would say. Its implementation would call for far-reaching changes both in the formal program and in the informal pattern of the church's educational functions, reversing their general impetus and turning them outward toward the world from their present institution-centered introversion. Is the church on the corner capable of such a radical change in orientation? Can its educational program ever be really effective in preparing the laity for their ministry in the world? The current debate on the issues posed by such questions as these constitutes the most comprehensive and significant questioning of the traditional and normative parish social structure in the long history of Christendom. These questions demand answers which in turn will determine the long-range strategy of Christian education.

Chapter III

The Local Church as Instrument for Renewal

MANY LEADERS and exponents of the recovery of the full ministry of the laity in the world both in Europe and in America are exceedingly skeptical about the potentialities of the local church for this kind of renewal. Some emphatically insist that this emphasis cannot be made into a program, that it implies not so much a program as an explosion. They say it is as impossible as putting new wine into old wineskins. Hendrik Kraemer notes, but with disapproval, the tendency of many creative lay movements both in Continental Europe and in North America to write off the empirical church as utterly hopeless because of its "introvert spirit and preoccupation."[13] In Europe, the revival of concern for the ministry of the laity in the world is centered in the many lay training centers commonly referred to as the Evangelical Academies, and a spirit of anti-institutionalism directed against the local church pervades most of these centers. Serious tensions and suspicions exist, on both sides, between the lay centers and the functionaries of the more traditional ecclesiastical organizations. There are recurring expressions of doubt coming from bishops, pastors, and board secretaries as to what good the exciting novelties of Bossey or Bad Boll will eventually accomplish within the routine of the local parish.

Speaking with regard to such lay centers as the Parishfield community in Michigan, Austin's Faith and Life community in Texas, and Agape in Italy, John Fry observes in his book *A Hard Look at Adult Christian Education* that "these experiments have strong anticlerical notions and are distinctly antiecclesiastical. They radiate good and almost cheerful destructiveness. Together they might, eventually, break down the huge bureaucratic bourgeois monolith bearing the name Protestant Church."[14] Far less bitterly anti-institutional than Fry's observations, but equally despairing of any significant renewal of a world-oriented lay ministry coming from the local church, is the viewpoint Gibson Winter advances in *The Suburban Captivity of the Churches*. Winter gives a devastatingly accurate description of the introverted "organization church" as he calls it, especially as it exists in suburbia and other residential enclaves. He accurately depicts its hyperactivism, its superficiality, its geographical and psychological insulation from most of the public concerns of life, and especially its insulation from the business and industrial communities of the metropolitan area. He then makes this gloomy evaluation of the neighborhood church as a locus for significant lay renewal: "The lay apostolate is foredoomed if its participation in the productive and political community is anchored in the segregated context of residential communities. We have seen ample evidence of this fact in lay movements based in residential enclaves, which invariably become large-scale facsimiles of the introverted activism of the organization church. With a few minor exceptions, this has been the fate of the lay movements which emerged in the American churches after World War II."[15] Winter argues that we must look, not to the local church, but to specialized "sector ministries" involving laymen all the way from exurbanite areas on in to a city's industrial and commercial core, and lay training centers for these sector ministries, to overcome the present dichotomy between the communities of production and the communities of consumption and residence. Only such paraparochial institutions, he argues, can successfully invigorate and direct a significant renewal of lay ministry in our urbanized society.

In *The New Creation as Metropolis,* his more recent book on the same general theme, Winter predicts that evangelical centers and academies will not be auxiliaries to the residential parish churches; instead, they will be the *normative* form of the church in our emerging metropolitan society.[16] In his opinion, the local church is utterly incapable of sustaining a ministry of Christian communication within the structures of government, community planning, and public administration, all of which are, of course, crucial areas for the church's witness. The training of the lay apostolate, Winter insists, must be carried on in the very places where the laity are engaged in their secular responsibilities. All talk of such forms of lay renewal being generated within local parishes inevitably "degenerates into one more organizational program of the religious enterprise,"[17] or else becomes swallowed up in the local parish's overwhelming preoccupation with privatized, familial interests, divorced from the public sphere. Christendom is hopelessly privatized in the scope of its collective concern, and is largely limited to family and residential neighborhood interests, so long as the local church is its primary institutional manifestion.

Winter argues for establishing the center of gravity for Christendom in new paraparochial structures that would parallel the industrial and political structures of the modern metropolis, with only quite secondary ministries to the more privatized spheres of family and neighborhood life through neighborhood parishes. He maintains that the prevailing direction of influence and social causation is from the community of work to the community of leisure, from the centers of production to the centers of consumption and residence, from daily work to family life, almost never the other way around. The neighborhood church and its constituent families, Winter believes, are essentially passive by their very nature. They are the objects, rather than the potential initiators, of significant social change. He declares that "experiences with direct ministries in industry suggest that there is a natural tendency for them to carry over into the more intimate contexts of the residential association. This is a very different matter, however, from the attempt to work out of the privatized spheres of residential association into the public spheres. The process does not work from private to public, because the pietistic tradition of American Christianity is simply reinforced and consolidated in the residential context."[18]

Winter's words constitute a welcome and much-needed corrective to programs of Christian family life education that seem to assume that just because the family is the basic social unit of human community, it is therefore almost totally determinative of the character and quality of human community, and that the problems of family life can be talked about without discussing the problems originating in external social forces that impinge upon the family. Any insight that has power to free leaders in the church from the sentimental illusion of essentially autonomous families able to examine the quality of their interrelationships in blissful abstraction from any significant consideration of environing economic and social factors is indeed welcome. But the verdict Winter summarily pronounces upon the local church itself cannot be so welcomed by anyone who has reason to believe that a meaningful program for the nurture of a lay apostolate can emerge from this residential base. If Winter is right, then Christendom's strategy of concentrating its human and financial resources on local churches rather than on paraparochial ministries to industry, commerce, and government ought to be completely reversed.

Winter speaks for many who are engaged in experimental ministries in industrial missions and lay academies and centers of various sorts, together with those most enthusiastically enamored of such ventures, who would relegate the local church to a very secondary role in Christian strategy. Many of these people believe that the clergy of the local churches cannot realistically aspire to any basically broader role than to serve as chaplains to the privatized interests of families and neighborhoods and strictly local social issues, and that the training of laymen for their public ministerial responsibilities, transcending their more private ministries to their spouses and children and immediate neighbors, constitutes an educational task for which the local church is almost by definition unsuited.

The same sort of pessimistic verdict on the possibilities inherent in the local church has been expressed by the foremost pioneer in ecumenical industrial mission, the Church of England's Bishop Wickham. Wickham, who began his famous industrial mission experiment in Sheffield during World War II, makes the following observation concerning the need for some institutional form other than the local parish church if the message of the gospel is to be intelligibly related to the industrial milieu:

> Some special agency of the church is required to be concerned with this expression of the Church's life and impact. The reasons are really very clear. The local church must be preeminently concerned with the *homes* of the parish and the building up of the Christian congregation, a many-sided task

that must take precedence in emphasis over the secular obedience of Christian men in the larger institutions of society. In heavily industrialized areas the proper sphere of that secular involvement will almost certainly fall outside the parish; the people one should work with will be scattered over a wide area, while the problems Christians have to grapple with are too specialized and technical to be dealt with in the parochial context.[19]

Speaking in a similar vein, Robert Spike in his book *Safe in Bondage* advocates a program of vocational evangelism, training men and women for effective witness through their personal relationships at work, with the recruitment of concerned persons being handled directly through the communities of business and industry rather than through local churches. Spike suggests that suburban churches combine their resources to provide specialized vocational ministers, who would not necessarily be clergymen, to be attached to the staffs of downtown churches because of their proximity to the world of work. He recommends the establishment of reading rooms and conference centers in these areas, and suggests that various denominations might concentrate their attention on certain industries and professions. Truly effective work with specialized vocational groupings, he believes, can only be achieved through interchurch effort.

The explicit and implied pessimism concerning the potentialities of the residentially oriented parish church that is being voiced by men like Winter and Wickham and Spike is impressive, even though these men are not voicing their opinions from within the present context of a parish pastorate. Far more telling, however, is the impact of similar opinions when voiced by men, presently serving as local pastors, who share the same sort of ideal vision of the church's mission as these prophetic critics. Not long ago Gordon Cosby, pastor of the small but world-famous

Church of the Savior in Washington, D.C., reported his despairing conclusions with regard to the local church:

> The present institutional structures of the church must give place to new structures that will *be* the church on mission. This conviction has come to me gradually—I have worked with it consciously for the past fifteen years and have been disturbed about it for the past three. Just a few weeks ago I crossed a line in my thinking. Now I am convinced that the institutional structures that we know are not renewable. Even when there is renewal (and this goes on in many congregations) the stance of the church almost always remains the same—a stance which is contrary to the very nature of a church committed to mission. . . . When the structures get as rigid and resistant to change as they are now, perhaps the wisest strategy is not to try to renew them. It may be wiser strategy to bypass them and let God do with them what He will. . . . One reason it has been so difficult for me to come to the conclusion stated above is that I, myself, came to know Jesus Christ through the old structures. This reproach has been thrown at me time and again, and it is true. So it is with great reluctance that I have to say that I do not believe that the old structures can be renewed.[20]

Cosby intends to continue accepting invitations to speak at seminaries and churches around the country but his avowed goal is no longer the renewal of old forms of congregational life but, rather, the radical reformation of the shape of the church in conformity with the largely nonresidential shape of the modern world of work and politics and leisure. Cosby's "agonizing reappraisal" of the local parish is particularly devastating in its impact because his unique experiment in gathering a congregation of highly disciplined and trained Christians for effective scattering as leaven in the nation's capital has for years now shone forth as a promising beacon of hope, an exemplary model of the possibilities for a regenerate and world-involved style of churchmanship. His conclusions of despair concerning present congregational structures therefore have an even sharper and more disturbing ring of authority than those of men existentially removed from parish experiments in renewal.

The most disturbing thing about the thoughtful recommendations coming from all these men, and many others who also might be mentioned, is not in the recommendations themselves, but in the assumption, whether explicit or implicit, that the local church really has nothing to contribute to the renewal of lay ministry except presumably the money to finance the paraparochial organizations they are championing. This assumption needs to be thoroughly examined before we consign the local church to a limbo of irrelevance.

In defense of their point of view, it must be admitted that the local church has a number of considerable handicaps which stand in the way of its carrying out an effective program of education for lay ministries in the world. For one thing, the gathered church in its local manifestation represents such a wide diversity of vocations that the general pattern of its worship and instruction can convey little that is specifically applicable to the specialized vocational situation of each lay member. This occupational diversity is usually so great that even a quite considerable number of specialized vocational study groups would fail to provide for more than a minority of a church's membership. The high ratio of laymen to clergy is in itself a considerable limitation if it is assumed that closer communication between clergy and laity is essential for this kind of renewal. The fact that church membership is increasing at a faster rate than the number of available pastors only aggravates this problem. And with the postwar church building boom, the expansion of church school enrollments, and similar manifestations of ecclesiastical growing pains, the church has found it easy to become so completely absorbed in the problems of its own institutional growth that it has had little time or energy left to concern itself much with the impact of the church upon the world. Moreover, it is very easy for the church to mistake its massive postwar popularity for success; and when the church has been successful without seriously engaging the secular order through its laymen, it is difficult for it to see any compelling reason why it should try to change its ways.

Even the geographical location of the typical neighborhood church in relation to where its people work is a not insignificant handicap. This handicap is well symbolized by the church bell. Before the industrial revolution, the church bells gave the signal for the farmer to rise for his early chores, and for the tradespeople to open their shops. As the author of Ecclesiastes says, there is an appointed time for everything under the sun, and the church bells kept time for the whole of life. Today, far fewer of the church's people perform their daily work within hearing range of the church bells. Except for the great downtown churches, many of which are in a state of serious decline because of the flight to the suburbs, the churches are far removed from the places where most of their people work. The church is associated in the minds of laymen with their place of residence rather than their place of work, with residential and family life rather than with work life. Geographical distance thus has contributed to a sense of psychological and spiritual distance for the laymen. Symbolically, as well as physically, the church bell is seldom heard where a man earns his daily bread.

The disadvantages intrinsic to the local church as a center for lay renewal are even further highlighted when compared with the corresponding advantages inherent in some of the lay centers and institutes. Whereas a large portion of the educational effort of the local church is necessarily directed toward leadership training to meet its own institutional needs, the educational work of the various lay centers can be directed wholly outward toward the layman's mission in the world. Industrial missions have the advantage not only of staff specialization, but also the ability to expend their energies entirely within the business and industrial orbit of great cities. The world of work can be defined as an ecumenical situation; men from different churches and denominations, as well as the unchurched who are indifferent or perhaps even hostile toward churches, work side by side.

An ecumenical approach to the work situation, freed of the handicaps of association with any particular church in the minds of the workers, harmonizes best with the natural ecumenical character of functional work relationships. Denominational labels constitute very real obstacles to the enlistment of co-workers in discussion groups. The ecumenical definition of industrial mission employed by staff persons in industrial mission obviates this problem, and at the same time vastly simplifies the problem of winning the confidence and consequent cooperation of management. Simply gaining access to certain places of work is a difficult enough task even for professional leaders in industrial mission, in spite of all their ecumenical credentials.

It must also be conceded that various lay institutes have demonstrated an ability to foster significant theological conversations with highly specialized lay groups that are simply beyond the realm of possibility for almost any particular church. The Ecumenical Institute at Bossey has convened artists and writers, and the program of the Community of Villemetrie in France has included groups of radio and television organizers, theatrical people, movie actors, and prominent leaders in scientific research. The lay centers provide a place for deliberate concentration on those aspects of life which are divorced from the ordinary life and thought of the local church, for those aspects within which men and women who are highly specialized vocationally need highly specialized opportunities that will help them find both themselves and the best form of their obedience under God.

Yet even when the advantages of the lay centers and missions and the contrasting disadvantages inherent in the local church have been admitted, the evidence scarcely seems to support the specious assumption of some enthusiasts that these paraparochial movements can and must achieve the rebirth of lay ministry single-handedly, and that the local church can do virtually nothing in this regard. Indeed, upon closer examination, some of the advantages of these movements over the local church turn out to be considerably less than absolute. For example, although, as we noted, the representatives of industrial missions can perhaps more easily gain physical access to particular places of work in commerce and industry, and gain the blessing or at least the tolerant acquiescence of management in the formation of such on-the-site contacts as interviews with individual workers and the gathering of lunch-hour discussion groups, it is nevertheless a fact that such dispensations are obtained by clergy lacking any explicitly ecumenical passport. (The author, identified simply as a Presbyterian pastor meeting with a luncheon group of laymen not all of whom are his parishioners, regularly is admitted, though under escort, to a very high-security plant having many defense contracts.) Furthermore, although a majority of workers do work together with other workers in the same place, at the same plant or office, a large proportion of workers who are engaged in similar or identical lines of employment are geographically scattered over a wide area in small work units, or even as solitary workers. This is true of many sales people and service people and self-employed professionals, to mention but a few such occupational categories.

Where there is no one place of work, no one corporation involved, the institutional advantages of an industrial mission in gaining access or in establishing contacts are considerably less important. Even the advantage that industrial missions enjoy in being able to assemble a close-knit group of fellow workers with a fairly specialized occupational common denominator with comparative ease is not an unqualified indication of greater potential effectiveness. Experience has shown that there are some advantages in forming discussion groups of people who do not normally confront one another in their work relationships. This may be especially true with regard to the superior-subordinate relationship, since evidently many men find it hard to talk openly and frequently in the presence of their own superior. And in regard to the lay institutes and schools of theology for laymen other than those which can be called industrial missions, it is noteworthy that a large portion of their course offerings and retreat schedules have nothing whatsoever to do with specialized vocational groupings but, instead, assemble interested persons for discussion centering around general themes of contemporary concern, such as Christianity and the arts, economic issues, the social impact of technological change, and the like. Local churches are not disadvantaged by any iron law of necessity as compared with the more specialized institutions when it comes to providing such vocationally generalized opportunities for lay education as these, or whenever the defined occupational spectrum is broad enough to include people from a number of firms or offices, or at least from different departments of one large enterprise.

There is a desperate need for constant two-way communication between the parish and the more specialized institutions dedicated to the renewal of lay ministry. These two forms of the church are essentially dependent upon each other. Unless there is some awakening at the grass roots, at the local level, the vast majority of Christians will remain unable even to comprehend what these exponents of renewal are talking about. As long as the local churches remain indifferent or apathetic toward the concerns embodied in these new experiments, the latter are in danger of engendering a new monasticism, far more isolated from the mainstream of modern Christendom than was the older monasticism from the mainstream of medieval Christendom.

These new institutional experiments in lay renewal are dependent in large measure on local churches both for their financial support and for lay persons interested in engaging in the kind of dialogue they exist to create. If the leadership in the local churches does not work to enable the people to hear what these experiments are trying to say, the whole effort may be foredoomed to the position of a splinter sect. That this has proved to be an ever-present danger on the German scene is indicated by Margaret Frakes in her book on the lay academy movement. Even in areas where the academies enjoy quite close and sympathetic ties with regional church authorities, not to mention those regions which regard the academies with official mistrust or indifference, there is the continuing paradox of new vitality and ever-increasing popular interest in the programs of the academies existing side by side with a parish system that seems to have been largely unaffected by all this new ferment.[21] The cause of this situation seems to lie in a lack of adequate intercommunication between the staffs of the academies and the pastors of local churches, with both largely to blame for the atmosphere of mutual aloofness. Although the American scene may not be characterized by a similar degree and kind of jealousy and suspicion between pastors and those in the "experimental ministries," there certainly is tension in some quarters of the pioneering denominations and a tragic degree of misunderstanding and sheer ignorance, particularly on the part of pastors, that is at least comparable to the European situation.

It is interesting to note some signs which indicate that leaders in the academy movement, as well as increasing numbers of parish pastors, are becoming aware of the dangers inherent in this general unwillingness of parish and academy to listen to what the other has to say. Dr. Klaus von Bismarck, director of the West German Broadcasting Service in Cologne, and a prominent lay leader in the German academy movement, not long ago made this observation: "The idea of para-churches (i.e., small decentralized mission-cells of the church which deliberately detach themselves from the General Market Place of the traditional church members) has proved to be merely utopian. Many of us have learned that contact with the body of our visible Church (with all its faults) is absolutely essential. Otherwise, we shall become anemic, isolated, detached limbs."[22]

There has been a distinct tendency among many lay centers and missions to concentrate on certain small policy-making elites among the laity, at least partly because of the obviously greater causal leverage on the affairs of the world that such elite groups possess. Hendrik Kraemer warns against this tendency, saying: "There often exists, amongst those who work hard at getting the lay issue in the right perspective, a dangerous tendency to think only in terms of a 'select' laity. Of course a certain minority of the laity, who possess great cultural and educational advantages or occupy important places in some sector of the world's life, have, if this is truly brought under the rule of Christ, special significance. But in the first place, the rule must stand that the whole laity matters, of whatever description, both the 'select' and the ordinary laity. Both are called."[23]

If, as Kraemer says, "the whole laity matters," and the New Testament clearly affirms that it does, then the local church itself must become a focal point for Christian education aimed at the rebirth of lay ministry. Because the whole laity matters, and because the lay centers and missions could never conceivably involve the whole laity, the ferment of the lay renaissance, in North America at least, must find principal lodgement in the life of the local church. It may be, as some say, that within a generation the religious situation of the American churches will closely resemble the current European picture. But whether or not that prophecy will prove to be correct, the present fact of the matter is that there are major cultural differences calling for major differences in strategies for renewal.

The imperative need for large numbers of lay training centers with large staffs and accommodations for sizable numbers of people is very evident in the case of European Christendom. In contrast with the popularity of the churches in America (however superficial and merely conventional that popularity may be), large segments of the European population feel utterly alienated from their parish churches. This is particularly true of manual workers, intellectuals, artists, and specialists in the mass media.

Such persons respond to invitations from the lay academies, especially when these invitations come indirectly through their employers or unions or professional associations, when in all likelihood such an invitation coming from a local parish church would evoke only a yawn or a sneer. Furthermore, the European parish churches often are so weak and moribund, so devoid of strong lay leadership after centuries of highly authoritarian dominance by the clergy, and the clergy themselves are so overtaxed because of their double role as pastors and as officers of the state keeping official government records of the births, marriages, and deaths for thousands of utterly nominal members on their parish rolls, that few of them would be in a position to present an appealing program of lay education in the first place.

No one would deny that we have much to learn from the lay developments in Europe in the postwar years. However, it must be recognized that the popularity and strength of Christianity in North America is centered in local congregations, in sharp contrast with the European situation. Conditions in Europe almost required that the local parish be bypassed if the church was to enter into meaningful dialogue with the world, and if the laity was to begin to discover its authentic Biblical identity and mission, at least during the early stages. By contrast, conditions in North America seem to require that the vast resources of the local church be directly and primarily utilized to achieve this same goal of lay renewal. In contrast with war-ravaged or antiquated facilities, North American church buildings are generally well equipped for lay education. In contrast with the European situation of paltry state stipends to the churches and little sense of individual responsibility for substantial financial support, together with a tradition of almost sheepish lay passivity in the churches' institutional life, and with the vast majority of the membership utterly nominal in their association with their churches, if not openly hostile, the American churches are at least relatively well endowed with financial resources, and with a long tradition of almost franticly activistic lay involvement both in the provision of leadership and in all other forms of institutional participation.

A cynic might argue that we would be better off if we could start where European Christendom started after the war, with bombed-out or decaying, moribund parish churches that could be easily ignored and dismissed as loci for the renewal of lay ministry. Perhaps it *would* be easier to start virtually from scratch, as the Europeans had to do, rather than to try to remake popular, prosperous, superficial St. Vitus Protestant Church into a focal point for significant lay training. But the cynics' arguments would only be wishful thinking, for the strength of the local parish structure is a reality, one of the most evident and cogent social realities in North American Christendom. No reasonable sense of stewardship over our available Christian resources will allow us to do anything but to accord to the local church a position of utterly central importance in any strategy of renewal.

The reasons that the Abbé Michonneau gives in his book, *Revolution in a City Parish,* as to why the local church cannot be bypassed, are even truer for American Protestantism than they are for the French Catholicism of which he was speaking:

> First, because it is already existing. Whether it plays its role or not, *hic et nunc,* the parish is a fact. It is, by right if not in reality, that tiny cell of Christianity of the Incarnation. . . . Not even the civil government is as well organized. . . . And that is not all, for a parish is equipped. It has its priests,

and parish clergy have always been the mainstay of the Church's force. They live in the midst of those whom they are evangelizing. They are, or can be, or should be in permanent contact with their people. . . . However forceful or generous or ingenious may be specialized methods, it will always be the parish which represents the main strength of the attack, like the infantry of an army. Like the infantry, it will be beaten if it fails to use new armaments and tactics, but it remains the indispensable means of holding any point of attack.[24]

Important as it is to say that we cannot afford to bypass the parish church and all its vast resources, Michonneau reminds us of an equally important truth concerning the church's need to modernize its armaments and tactics. This means that the leadership of the local church must have the humility to learn from the creative experiments constantly being carried out in the lay centers, to regard them, so to speak, as laboratories for lay renewal. Unfortunately there is as yet relatively little literature emanating from these centers, but what little there is should be studied by local leadership, however tentative the conclusions it contains may be. Hendrik Kraemer points to this need for the local church to learn and profit from these experiments when he declares that "the 'first fruits' of fraternities, house-churches, para-parochial congregations, retreats (not for retreat's sake, but for the sake of going out into the world) etc. should not continue to exist alongside the Church. They should be acknowledged as really doing *the* business of the Church, also the institutional Church. All these pioneer movements should not be left to the imaginative inventiveness of those individuals who took the initiative, but adventuring in these directions should become also the concern of the Churches, because they are reminders of what the Church really exists for."[25]

Many churches are too far removed geographically to profit from these paraparochial centers of renewal except through that small trickle of literature which flows sporadically from them. But many others are close enough to engage in conversation with them, especially by having clergy and representative laymen involved in some of the groups they gather. For example, the Ecumenical Institute in Evanston, Illinois, brings together members of various professional groups, drawn largely from local parishes, to consider the problems of their vocations in the light of the Christian faith. Clergy and laymen from churches in the area are often gathered for mutual discussion on the role of religion in modern life. The Detroit Industrial Mission has worked in even closer and more continuous association with four representative parish churches in the metropolitan Detroit area. The activity of the Mission staff varied from parish to parish, and included such things as preaching, helping laymen to discuss and criticize a Sunday sermon, leading adult study groups, and exploring with a group of salesmen what Christianity means for their daily work. Significant cross-fertilization of ideas took place when the clergy of the four parishes met with the Mission staff bimonthly for theological study. Quite obviously, this has served to keep the Mission close to church life at the grass-roots level.

Even more examples of this kind of close liaison between paraparochial organizations and local parishes are to be found in the Roman Catholic Church. The Catholic lay renaissance in the United States surpasses Protestant movements both in its output of literature and in the breadth and scope of its activities. It also seems to have a more consistent and widespread awareness of the fact that a beginning must be made at the parish level, and thus the initial objective is to create a vigorous congregational life. Cana conferences, designed to help engaged couples and husbands and wives to understand more fully the nature and responsibilities of Christian marriage, and more specialized lay movements, such as the Catholic Rural Life Conference, various vocational guilds, and the Catholic Worker Movement, all operate in very close association with parish churches.

"Pre-Cana conferences" for engaged couples, preferably at least six months before their marriage, and the "Tri-Cana conferences" involving teen-agers together with their parents, are organized and conducted at the parish level. The same is very often true of the Cana conferences for couples presently married. Ordinarily a Cana conference will involve around forty or fifty couples from the same parish for one full day, or perhaps one long afternoon. It is conducted by a priest who has been specially trained for Cana conference leadership under diocesan auspices, and an attempt at least is made to talk about Christian attitudes toward such diverse and secular factors in marriage as daily work, education, and finances, in addition to the more predictable subjects such as family piety or the role of sex in marriage. The Cana movement is centered around a concern for the renewal of that aspect of the lay apostolate which is to be exercised in marriage. One of its explicit objectives is to help the Roman Catholic laity to see marriage as a *continuing* sacrament and as an important aspect of the lay person's "vocation."[26] The Cana movement is now nationwide, and is even being imitated abroad. Although the strength of the movement varies widely from one diocese to another, it is influential in large segments of American Catholic life because this strength is largely concentrated in metropolitan dioceses and archdioceses. The Chicago Archdiocese alone has annually over six thousand couples involved in Cana conferences, and over seven thousand engaged couples participating in Pre-Cana conferences, representing nearly one half of all Catholics getting married in that archdiocese.

Another significant venture in training for the lay apostolate which has its center of gravity in the local parish is the Christian Family Movement, a part of Catholic Action. Like the Cana movement, CFM is particularly vigorous around metropolitan areas such as Buffalo, Chicago, Fort Wayne, and Portland, Oregon. It has as its objective the renewal of Christian family life in its totality through the formation of neighborhood inquiry groups, and nothing that affects the family—politics, economics, recreation, or art—is foreign to its concern.[27] A CFM unit normally consists of four or five neighbor couples meeting in one another's homes. The parish priest serves as chaplain-adviser and resource person to the group. Following the manual prepared for them, the groups proceed according to the three steps that are virtually the motto of Catholic Action with regard to all social problems: (1) observe a given social situation; (2) judge or evaluate it by Christian doctrinal standards; and (3) then act. The program format for a meeting includes discussion of passages from the Gospels guided by the manual, followed by a period of "social inquiry" set out in the manual lessons and centering upon such topics as economic life, work in modern society, schooling (including school integration and educational provisions for retarded children), sex, and public health.[28]

It is significant and instructive to note that this Roman Catholic material for Christian family life education, in contrast with most Protestant material prepared for parents' use, seeks to strengthen Christian family life through improving the layman's understanding of the vast social forces that so largely shape the family's ways of living, and through constantly encouraging Christian social action on his part to ameliorate these environing social conditions. Whereas Protestant materials tend to concentrate on matters confined to the privatized life of the home, such as child-centered psychologizing, answering questions children ask, informal Christian education in the home, and family devotional practices, the materials prepared by Catholic Action seek to relate questions of family life to the realities of the family's social milieu. In this regard as well as in others, the Protestant churches can profit from paying serious attention to the literature of the Catholic lay renaissance in this country, and especially from perceiving the wisdom of its insistence that the local parish must be the major locus for lay renewal, with various paraparochial institutions challenging, advising, and stimulating the local parish to this end.

The local church, with all its limitations and liabilities, is admittedly ill-suited for the task of Christian education for lay renewal. Its geographical insularity, its general self-centered institutional introversion even beyond that considerable amount of institutional self-maintenance which is absolutely essential to its existence, and the vast diversity of occupations represented in its membership all constitute formidable handicaps. However, God's call to mission in and to the world is a call addressed to the whole church, including its entire laity. It is admirable that through the work of the experimental, pioneering vanguard of the various lay institutes and centers a small minority has already begun to hear and to respond to this call. This minority can and already is exercising a limited leavening influence. But the whole church will be enabled to hear this divine summons to total mission only if it is mediated through the leadership of the local church. Furthermore, only the local church has the capability of educating more than a relative handful of the laity for their ministry in the world.

By any objective assessment, as we have said, the local church seems quite ill-suited for this task. By the same token, it can be said that objectively considered, God in Biblical history chose a nation that was ill-suited for the task he gave it, not to mention the many seemingly ill-suited individuals he summoned to specific tasks of leadership amid this people. The really crucial fact, however, was not this people's limitations, but the fact that God was calling them to mission in his world. The same is true of the people of God today, in its visible manifestation in the local church. Its suitability is secondary to the fact that God summons it to obedient witness and service in the world. The basic question is not one of asking whether or not the local church is adequately equipped to succeed in its task. The negative answer that must be given to that question, if considered alone, would only lead us to despair. Instead, the proper question concerns what shall be the form of the local church's obedience to its summons to call and educate its people for their unique ministries of penetration and involvement in the world. Our summons is not to some predetermined measure of success, but to obedience where we are and with what resources we have.

Chapter IV

Turning a Church Inside Out

IN HIS BOOK *We Shall Re-build*, Dr. George MacLeod, of Scotland's Iona Community, tells an oft-quoted story of a church that became turned around, or turned inside out. In Liverpool, on a prominent height of land overlooking the marketplace and the river Mersey with its heavy merchant ship traffic, stands the old parish church of St. Nicholas. Before the Second World War, the architectural orientation of the sanctuary was away from the river and the marketplace. To enter it meant turning your back on the busy river and marketplace, symbolic of all the bustle and creativity of modern secular life, and to find yourself peering at a distant Communion table in the gloomy light that passed through very heavy old stained glass. But the war changed all that. The church was hit during a bombing raid. It left the porch still standing, together with the tower, but the Gothic walls were left open to the elements. The stained-glass windows at the chancel end were smashed, and a charred cross marked where the old Communion table had stood. But because of the insight of an imaginative rector, a new small church emerged amidst the ruin and rubble. A prefabricated hut of very modern design was built, with only one tenth the original seating capacity; but it was built to face the other way. The surviving porch became the sanctuary, and the massive doors opening onto the old narthex became the windows of the new chancel, with no stained glass, looking out on the marketplace and the river.[29] As Dr. MacLeod indicates, this is a parable of drastic reorientation outward toward the world such as the church today desperately needs. The local church is, as we have seen, largely turned in upon itself. The posture of its people is a collective representation of what Luther was talking about when he spoke of the unredeemed heart as being "turned in toward itself." What is called for is a radical about-face, a turning around of the people to face the world and to perceive their God-given mission within it. In Biblical terminology, such a turning around is called "repentance." It is incumbent upon the church to sound such a call to repentance. Someone has aptly said that every Christian stands in need of two conversions: the first to Christ, and the second back to the world again. The call to repentance, for the sake of the Christian's "second conversion" to the world, must be addressed to everyone in the church.

Preaching

Preaching is the one way in which this call may be communicated to all. It is fashionable in many circles today, however, to minimize the effectiveness of preaching as a vehicle for changing men's behavior and attitudes. The findings of social psychologists have indeed made us aware of the limitations inherent in preaching as an instrument of significant personal change. These findings constitute a needed corrective against the too-sanguine expectations that many have traditionally attached to preaching. As an educational method, preaching has about the same handicaps as lecturing. Nevertheless, preaching does educate. It does communicate meanings within its methodological limitations. It does bring about some profound changes in both behavior and attitudes, even though not to as great an extent as earlier generations were prone to believe.

Yet to say too much either pro or con concerning the effectiveness of preaching is to fall into the pragmatic trap of making an idol of success. Just as the church as a whole is called primarily to be obedient rather than to be successful in its mission, so the individual preacher is called to proclaim the Word obediently regardless of what degree of "success" may ensue. Whatever the inherent limitations in the effectiveness of preaching, it is the one way in which the call to repentance, the call for an about-face toward the world, may be heard by everyone in the church. Whatever its degree of effectiveness, it is the one means by which every person in the church is forced to make a decision, to say either yes or no to the Word of God which calls him to discipleship within the secular order. Preaching on this issue of lay ministry in and to the world creates for all who hear it the moment of judgment. It says, in effect: "Behave yourself according to the divine privilege and calling in which you stand and are set, or else acknowledge before God your unbelief. Accept your call to ministry implicit in the fact of your baptism and membership in Christ's church, or else repudiate it. Choose you this day whom you shall serve." As Hendrik Kraemer has rightly said, "The essential nature of the Church has incessantly to be presented and interpreted in various tones to the *whole* membership, for only then the right division of light and dark becomes manifest, and the response can be continually purged."[30] Quite obviously this direct confrontation of the whole membership occurs only through preaching. Thus, whatever its intrinsic shortcomings as a means of communication, preaching can be universally effective in communicating the necessity of some decision concerning the totality of the Christian call to mission.

The summons to decision concerning this call should be implicit in preaching. But preaching on this subject, as on any other, properly begins with what God has done and is doing, as Scripture and present events perceived in the light of Scripture bear witness. Only then is preaching in a position to indicate what men should decide to be and do in response to God's activity. Biblical preaching at its best does not begin by dispensing abstract principles and ideals, but by pointing to God's action as revealed in Biblical history, and then by logical extension from this past revelation, pointing to indications of his present action in human events. It is the function of preaching to help people to see that God is already at work in their world. In their present parochial-mindedness, they are prone to think of his activity only within the gathered fellowship of the church, only when two or three are gathered in his name, and not when those same two or three are scattered in the world in his name. Preaching should help them to see not only what *God* is already doing in his world but also what *they* may already be doing in his world without being theologically conscious of it, as cocreators with God and as ambassadors or agents of his reconciling work among men.

Jesus' parable of the last judgment, in which the righteous are dumbfounded when told that they have been serving Christ in their kindness to their fellowmen, is a parable also of lay people's present need for inspiring enlightenment concerning the ultimate sacredness of many of their secular commitments and actions. They must be told who they already are within the divine economy, that they already are God's ministers by virtue of their membership in the church, however faithlessly they may presently be regarding or performing this ministry. Only then does it mean anything to challenge them to become in fact what they already are in principle. Biblical faith first testifies to an "is," and only then does it become power for an "ought." It declares how things presently are between God and man, before it introduces the "therefore" of appropriate Christian response.

Preaching can be most helpful in enabling lay people to see the relationship between worship and work. It can communicate the conception of the Christian life as an alternating rhythm between worship and work, between their two kinds of service: their praise of God through worship in the New Testament sense of liturgy as literally the "people's work" in worship, and their glorifying of God through their diaconate as service in the world. Preaching can help them see that which presently they so often fail to see, namely, the relationship between the encounter with God in public worship and other encounters with God in the world. It can make them aware that Sunday is not merely the end of the weekend, but Scripturally and symbolically the first day of a week that ends out in the world, not in the church. It can help them interpret their experiences of worship and instruction as preparatory to their secular life, viewing the church as a kind of home base from which they obtain supplies, refreshment, and training in tactics for their return to battle on the front line of their daily responsibilities.

There is one area of the people's ministry in the world outside the institutional church where preaching can go even farther and give fairly specific guidance. This area, quite obviously, is that of people's ministry to one another within another institution: the family. Sermons on Christian family life have the distinct advantage of allowing the preacher to be quite specifically helpful without shutting out any sizable portion of his hearers, in most congregations at least. Such sermons can be relevant to the lay ministry of nearly all who hear them. This cannot be said of any other area of lay ministry, with the exception of sermons on lay responsibility in social issues. There is just too wide a diversity in the other dimensions of lay responsibility represented in a congregation for the sermon to address them all specifically. But if preaching can help people perceive the fact that they do indeed have a ministry within their family relationships, and can constructively help them in that ministry, then preaching achieves a very significant point of penetration. It opens a door through which people may begin to be made aware of other ministries, outside the narrow sphere of family relationships, which are theirs as well.

It is the creation of this kind of openness and perceptual sensitivity that is probably the most significant fruit of preaching on the layman's mission. Persistent and well-conceived reiteration of this theme and its variations does not simply force the issue and evoke either the "no" of unfaith or the "yes" of faith. More than that, those whose response is affirmative will be turned around, "converted" so as to perceive their responsibilities in the world from the perspective of their stance within the gathered church at worship. As they thus face outward toward the world, preaching can point with specific relevance to only a few of these responsibilities in terms of concrete guidance, namely, in family life and certain social issues. No more than this need be asked or expected of the preaching function. When preaching accomplishes this much, when it succeeds in orienting those who respond to it outward toward the world in openness and expectancy, it has made a most important achievement. For it will then have created in many a desire for guidance and training for these newly discovered ministries, either from other educational opportunities in the church besides preaching or from the Holy Spirit at work in the world, through whom God reveals his specific will to those who earnestly seek it.

Special Programs and Projects

Quite aside from the potentiality of preaching, there are innumerable other ways in which to begin to turn a parish inside out, away from its introverted orientation. A number of creative and imaginative suggestions made by some of the leading exponents for the renewal of the ministry of the laity are worthy of mention. George Webber, of the East Harlem Protestant Parish, deplores the current exclusive stress on the clergyman as the one pastoral counselor, declaring that in every congregation there are men and women gifted with compassion and sensitivity who would be superb pastors and burden bearers. He feels that the clergy should release those with such gifts of the Spirit from parish busywork, and direct and train them to share in the work of counseling.[31] Gibson Winter, in *The Suburban Captivity of the Churches,* suggests that suburban churches might begin to break out of their captivity by involving some of their laymen in joint work with churches of the inner city, including special work on denominational and interdenominational commissions and boards that bridge sectional boundaries. Surely there should be far more of this kind of involvement on the part of suburban churches than there is. Established suburban churches, often richly endowed with highly capable lay leadership because of the high level of education and vocational proficiency represented in their memberships, are eminently capable of staffing entire church schools on a lend-lease basis for inner-city churches or new church developments, or of assisting in neighborhood censuses, to cite two possible examples. Admittedly, such forms of lay involvement still constitute only "church work" in the ecclesiastical sense; but they nevertheless would serve to break a congregation loose from its introverted geographical insularity, and would lay the groundwork for an even broader conception of the meaning of the lay apostolate to the modern city.

Robert Spike even sees a ray of hope for, of all things, the men's club. He suggests that since men's work life in offices and plants is often fraught with conflict and poor communication, a church might plan a series of men's meetings to explore the inner causes of conflict and the requirements for good communication. Occasionally, men's program meetings can become springboards to creative Christian social action, particularly when the local lay leadership is encouraged in this direction. A men's meeting with a program on alcoholism in one Presbyterian church in the Southwest generated enough interest to warrant the creation of a special study and action committee. This committee in turn led the church to invite a local Alcoholics Anonymous group to use the church's recreation rooms for their meetings and other activities, to encourage the school board to set up a realistic program of alcohol education in the high schools of the community, and to cooperate with other groups in the community in working to establish an information center on alocholism and improved rehabilitation facilities.

The men's organization of a church might also be the logical sponsor for programs to increase the political literacy and involvement of people in the community. But whoever might best serve as its sponsor, an open citizens' forum on current issues is one of the most effective means of instilling a less introverted image of the church's essential posture in the minds of people in the community at large as well as among the immediate membership. The immediate purpose of such forums is to expose persons to the views of the candidates and to the pros and cons of bond issues, operating levies, referenda, charter amendments, and other similar questions that are to be put to the electorate. Although there may occasionally be ballot questions or even particular candidates concerning which a church feels constrained to take sides, ordinarily a sponsoring church would simply be endeavoring to serve as a neutral catalyst for orderly and informative political dialogue, providing an opportunity for the various sides of often emotionally charged issues to come together in open and honest discussion. Sometimes, in certain communities at least, other organizations or institutions than the church may have made such adequate provision for this kind of political enlightenment that sponsorship of a citizens' forum by a church or a group of churches would be quite superfluous. However, it would seem that such situations of adequacy are the exception, and that in most communities and on many issues the churches have an opportunity, indeed a mandate created by the default of other groups, to serve the God of all truth by providing for the common enlightenment of all his children on impending political decisions that will have profound social effects.

Ernest Southcott in *The Parish Comes Alive* tells of a forum conducted in his church in Leeds, England, just before the general elections of 1950. After an opening prayer and the reading of Scripture, the Labor and Tory candidates for Parliament were alloted twenty minutes each for their presentations, concluding with a question period during which questions were addressed to them alternately. To everyone's amazement, it was discovered that the candidates had to be introduced to each other!

Not until they met in a parish hall had any portion of the electorate been provided with an opportunity to hear issues being directly debated by their candidates.[32] Similarly, not long ago in my own community a proposal for a city charter form of government was prepared at considerable expense and mailed to the voters, but with no provision for public discussion of its relative advantages and disadvantages. If the committee on social education and action of my church had not hastily arranged a forum consisting of members of the charter committee and city council, conducted on our premises for the benefit of the entire community, I am quite sure that our citizens would have had no such opportunity at all before going to the polls to determine a matter of most far-reaching importance for the community.

In Wilton, Connecticut, the Ecumenical Centre, which is sponsored by the Episcopal, Congregational, Methodist, Presbyterian, and Quaker churches of the town, joined with the Roman Catholic parish in sponsoring a public meeting on a highly controversial local referendum proposal to decide whether or not the town should provide transportation of pupils at public expense to the new Roman Catholic parochial school. Other towns in Connecticut facing this same issue of local option resolved it only after deep and bitter controversy which left community relations torn and mangled. But in Wilton, following the well-attended and well-ordered open debate sponsored by the churches, the tense, emotional atmosphere surrounding the issue gave way to a more dispassionate examination of the facts involved. Although the referendum to provide bus transportation was defeated, it was done without rending the total fabric of community relations and without leaving an aftermath of bitterness. Here again, if the church had not acted, the people would have remained in darkness, not to mention the social rifts which this reconciling ministry of the church helped to obviate.

The church has been entrusted with a ministry of reconciliation to the entire world; and one of the ways of exercising this ministry is to see to it that matters of conflict and controversy are aired in an atmosphere in which fair and orderly dialogue is a possibility. The God whose eye is upon each sparrow that falls, and who has numbered each hair on our heads, has a will, has a preference, between all the possible choices and combinations of choices with which elections confront the voter. Since God has a preferential will in these matters, since the uniqueness of each historical person and alternative prevents their being equally pleasing in his infinitely concerned sight, it behooves his church to cast as much light as possible on every facet of every political choice, both for its own membership and for the wider community that it is likewise called to serve. The light that is thereby thrown not only illuminates the public issues; it also reveals the church's outgoing concern for the totality of man's communal existence, and "teaches" to all a definition of the church's mission that will help to disabuse many people of the notions they may have concerning the church's institutional self-centeredness.

Stewardship Education

The nature of a church's program of stewardship education also is important in shaping attitudes concerning the church's relationship to the world. In the training of stewardship canvassers, in preaching on stewardship, and in the literature prepared by the church for the annual financial canvass, a self-centered institutional image of the church can be effectively challenged and changed. This reeducation can be effected if the training, the preaching, and the literature employed in communicating stewardship concepts will simply make explicit what is theologically assumed by many of the most thoughtful leaders of the churches: that support given to humanitarian and educational enterprises outside the institutional framework of the church, such as community-wide united appeals and alumni funds, generally serve the same redemptive purposes for which the church ideally exists. It is foolish for high-minded church leaders to regard this as so self-evident as to need no articulation or reiteration, for opinion and attitude surveys indicate that most people do not assume any such thing with regard to the church's aims. Furthermore, it is quite likely that even those few people who are theologically sensitive enough to have some grasp of the breadth and inclusiveness of the Biblical understanding of stewardship responsibility nevertheless interpret their church's silence concerning this broader meaning as a silence motivated by institutional self-interest. Even the word "stewardship" itself must be rescued from the semantic straitjacket in which custom and institution-centered promotionalism have placed it for so many, whereby it usually means to people nothing but the giving of time, talents, and money to the institutional church.

The various means of communication that the church utilizes for promotional purposes can be directed toward broadening people's sense of stewardship commitment as effectively and easily as they have been used in the past to deepen it within narrower grooves. This is not to imply that certain words by themselves, whether printed or spoken, are going to effect some magic alchemy that will suddenly transform a congregation's ways of thinking about the inclusiveness of what is meant by Christian stewardship. Nevertheless, if the verbalizing of the Biblical conception of stewardship as including every facet of responsibility to one's neighbor under God is even half as effective as the church's conspiracy of virtual silence along these lines has been negatively effective, it would amount to an educational accomplishment of major proportions.

A case can be made for including support for political as well as educational and humanitarian causes as part of what is meant by Christian stewardship. For if the strategy for effective witness in a democracy calls for membership and functional involvement in a political party as part of a Christian's responsibility, it is hard to see why the commitment of money as well to partisan purposes should not be included in the definition of Christian stewardship in which the church endeavors to educate its people. The fact that the Internal Revenue Service does not presently allow us to take income tax deductions for such political contributions under *their* definition of "charities" in no way prohibits us from including them in our *Christian* definition of "charity"; for surely one of the most effective and appropriate ways in which a person is able to show his "charity," his Christian love for his neighbor near or far, is through his influence on the political decision-making process. In addition, of course, the Biblical conception of stewardship includes responsibility for the way one spends and saves as well as gives his money, not to mention responsibility for the way he earns it in the first place. But presently the word "stewardship" needs to be rescued from a narrowly and almost literally "parochial" definition just in the dimension of giving quite aside from these other even broader dimensions of the word's meaning.

The Biblical means of giving is proportionate giving, or tithing; and however the tithe or proportion is defined, the church should encourage its people to include their giving to other at least potentially redemptive causes in arriving at the total proportion of their income which is to be set aside for that particular aspect of a Christian's stewardship which involves the giving of his money. Once lay people have recovered from the initial shock of hearing this kind of advice and exhortation coming from their financial canvass committees and their clergy, the way would be paved for a far more affirmative and therefore Christian attitude toward voluntary commitments to worthwhile causes within the secular order.

In shaping people's conceptions of the meaning of stewardship, the church goes about the task of winning commitments of time and ability in a way that is perhaps at least as important as the way it seeks financial commitments. Within recent years the churches have been increasingly successful in broadening the general understanding of the meaning of stewardship so as to include time and talents as well as money. They have been notably less effective in helping people to see that the commitment of time and ability in civic, cultural, and humanitarian service in the public realm is also an important part of the meaning of Christian stewardship. This failure is not attributable to any particular effort made by the churches but, rather, to what they have failed to do. Here, as in the case of financial support for worthwhile secular involvements, the root cause has been the churches' conspiracy of virtual silence concerning secular service, coupled with a heavy emphasis centered upon the needs of the institutional church for all manner of workers and officers.

One of the effective means by which many churches have broadened the general conception of Christian stewardship so as to include the commitment of time and ability has been to develop a systematic program of enlistment for service to the church. When people join the church, and periodically thereafter, they are asked to offer or pledge some portion of their time as well as of their money to volunteer church work. This worthy device, which has been employed so effectively to expand the generally understood meaning of stewardship, can be utilized to expand it still further. Reuel Howe suggests that a point of focus for all adult church membership courses should be the questions: When you become a member of the church, how are you going to exercise your ministry in the world? How and where does one serve Christ in the world? Such an approach has intriguing possibilities. It would carry us far beyond the present practice in church membership classes of merely making a pitch for the "stewardship of time and talents," narrowly conceived as simply signing people up for church chores.

The usual printed form that is used for the enlistment of church members' time and talents presents a quite exhaustive checklist of church jobs. It would help in the development of a more adequate conception of Christian stewardship through secular responsibilities as well as ecclesiastical responsibilities if checklists were to be used that would include categories such as public office and civic dutes, leadership in educational organizations or trade unions or professional associations, and similar forms of useful service to society. Not only would such an enlistment form be an effective means of indirectly teaching people to see their stewardship responsibility in a more inclusive light; it would also be helpful to those who are responsible for the selection and recruitment of lay workers to meet the church's personnel needs. In choosing personnel for various duties, a church's personnel development committee ought to take into consideration not only the expressed willingness and past experience of each church member, but also the nature and the extent of that member's secular involvements. It is just possible that such involvements in certain instances might appear to a perceptive personnel development committee to be a far more important form of lay ministry for the church member in question than the particular church job for which he is being considered.

Perhaps some personnel and nominating committees can be brought to see that although the New Testament calls the church the beloved bride of Christ, it adds that God loves the whole world also; and that God's creative and redemptive purposes in the world may better be served if the institutional church does not try to monopolize all the time and energies of those highly competent men and women whose exceptional abilities are recognized and competitively courted by the world as well as by the church. In certain situations, committees may be led to realize that it may not necessarily be God's will that the very best man be appointed or nominated for a given position in the church. It might be that the potentially "best" man's resources of time and energy should not be drained away from his crucial opportunity for ministry in a struggle for power in a trade union, or campaigning for a school board election, or his need to have a decent amount of time to spend with his family, and that the "second-best" man might well be the best man in God's sight for the church position.

If the church will periodically solicit some sort of broadly inclusive combination of present survey and future pledge concerning its people's responsible commitment of their time, and if the church's nominating and recruiting committees will utilize this information following the guidelines of an adequate theology of the church's calling to be a servant-people in God's world, then the proclamation of this kind of theology from the pulpit will receive a practical and corroborative reinforcement that will contribute to a more effective reeducation of the laity concerning the total scope of Christian stewardship.

Nonresidential Calling

One means of breaking down the layman's tendency to identify the church and its concerns merely with his residential enclave is through the pastor's presence in that part of the city where his men work. Some wit has said that life is a football game, with the men out on the gridiron while the pastor is up in the grandstand, explaining the game to the ladies. This is all too true of the usual pattern of parish calling, where the "parish" is narrowly defined as the place of residence. Clergy who have worked out a schedule of luncheon get-togethers with some of their laymen, either singly or in handfuls, not simply to talk about church business but about their men's business, have found the effort richly rewarding. Men often open up to an amazing extent in such situations, expressing their feelings of guilt, their resentments, and their satisfactions in connection with their work. Besides the broader conception of the church's concern and ministry that such conversations can communicate, they sometimes help to lay the groundwork for the formation of specialized vocational groups for the furtherance of creative dialogue between Christian affirmations and the problems of work.

Children's and Youth Work

Communicating the meaning of the Christian's calling in the world is properly an important concern of those who work with children and youth. It should be a point of focus for the entire educational program of the church, not simply for adult education. The ingenuous openness and receptivity of children and youth to the idealism of Christian conceptions of the meaning of work, in contrast with the more constricted attitudes toward daily work commonly held by adults, affords promising opportunities for nurture. Those who scoff at kindergarten or primary curriculum materials which stress the functions of all sorts of people from firemen to milkmen as "God's helpers" simply reveal their blindness to the value of such materials as a means of communicating a sense of Christian worth and dignity to even the most menial forms of work. Of course, this kind of emphasis is even more important with young adolescents who are beginning to make basic vocational decisions, although a curricular background from the lower grades is of obvious value in setting the stage for it. The majority of social and cultural influences brought to bear on young people in making vocational choices center around such criteria as the social status or potential earning power connected with various vocations.

Middle-class values and assumptions so thoroughly permeate our culture that even when parents and educators are careful to say nothing disparaging concerning those who work mainly with their hands, youngsters are keenly aware of the preferential valuation our society gives to white-collar work, and consequently the higher status accorded college preparatory as compared with commercial courses in high school. The educational program of the church should constitute a counterweight to these influences, confronting youth with Christian considerations of one's potential service to God in the world as a basic criterion. The nationwide survey conducted by the Office of Family Education Research of The United Presbyterian Church U.S.A. showed that parents are deeply concerned that the church's program with youth include this emphasis. The parents in the survey were asked to list eight topics for family life education that they would like to see implemented in the church's program. "A Christian Interpretation of Vocation," primarily directed at youth, was listed third out of the eight, being outvoted only by the topics of parent-child relations and boy-girl relations in adolescence.

The churches have a crucial opportunity and responsibility at this point, partly by default, and partly by constitutional necessity. There are relatively few communities around the country that can be said to be doing a fully adequate job of providing vocational guidance to their young people. The increasing popularity of "career days," often jointly sponsored by the schools and by other community organizations, has had some salutary effects in confronting young people with a general picture of the requirements and possibilities inherent in various lines of work. However, these short periods of emphasis almost never provide for individual conferences with the men and women who represent the different occupations. And even when the ratio of students to high school guidance counselors is low enough to provide some modicum of individual attention, this can scarcely be the equivalent of conferring with an adult who is actually trained and engaged in the line of work the student is considering. Furthermore, no matter how good a school's vocational guidance program may be from a technical and pedagogical standpoint, our constitutional separation of church and state necessitates that this guidance not be presented in the context of an explicit and articulated Christian philosophy of vocation. Thus the mandate to the churches is obvious.

For a number of years now the Presbyterian Church U.S. has been conducting an ambitious program of vocational guidance in a Christian context. At the level of the local church, the plan centers on the work of laymen referred to as "vocational aides," whose function it is to meet several times with three to five high school sophomores who are interested in the same vocational field as the vocational aide's or one similar to it. These interviews normally are spread over the whole of a student's tenth school year. The completion of these spaced interviews qualifies a young person for recommendation and referral to a regional Presbyterian Guidance Center, for a short but intensive period of interviews and analytical testing. Although this is a denomination-wide program, its all-important starting point is the series of interviews with the adult laymen in the local church who serve as vocational aides. The interviews they conduct are informal conferences, designed to help each student understand that the occupation he is considering can be a primary mode of his lay ministry, and to encourage him to learn more about his own talents and about today's complex world of work.[33]

A similar kind of counseling program is within the competence of other churches as well. Indeed, it could be argued that such a counseling opportunity, offered during either the sophomore or junior year of high school, should be part of the curriculum of preparation of every young person for ministry in the world of work. If care is exercised in the selection of counselors in terms of the maturity of their Christian commitment and psychological fitness for conducting counseling interviews, very little formal training and orientation for this task would be required. Actually, such interviews as these should be essentially a more individualized and personalized variation of that confrontation with the Christian understanding of vocation which begins in earnest at the junior high level in the communicants class and the youth fellowship program. Church-sponsored vocational counseling at the high school level ought to be part of a cumulative learning experience, building upon earlier exposures to the meaning of the Christian doctrine of work. The reason for special curricular emphasis upon this at approximately the eighth-grade level and again at the eleventh-grade level should be obvious. Each of these grade levels immediately precedes in most public-school systems the two stages of an enormously significant vocational channeling process. At the first stage, the eighth- or ninth-grader must choose between the two general categories of college or noncollege occupational possibilities in the selection of a general course of studies. A survey study of various occupations is quite often a part of the public school curriculum at this grade level to provide background for the decision between the "college preparatory" and "commercial" course of studies. The second stage in this process of selection comes when the high school junior or senior faces an even more narrowing choice between specific types of colleges or different kinds of commercial training. Curricular concentration on the theme of Christian vocation in the church's educational program at these two critical junctures thus serves to provide a Christian framework and value system just at the time when impending decisions allow Christian affirmations concerning the meaning of work to be heard as answers to very real and pressing questions in the minds of youth.

The general Christian commitment toward which a church's total youth program should seek to guide its young people, regardless of what particular occupation they may eventually enter, has been aptly phrased in a statement prepared many years ago by the student department of the Y.M.C.A. It is called "A Christian's Fundamental Life Work Decision."

"I will live my life under God for others rather than for myself, for the advancement of the Kingdom of God rather than my personal success.

"I will not drift into my life work, but will do my utmost by prayer, investigation, meditation, and service to discover that form of life work in which I can become of the largest use to the Kingdom of God.

"As I find it I will follow it under the leadership of Jesus Christ, wheresoever it takes me, cost what it may."

This is the kind of general decision about the Christian significance of one's life that the youth of the church should be challenged to make, preceding any specific vocational decision.

The conviction of being called to a ministry in the world in and through vocational commitment need not and should not have merely a future reference for youth. The youth program of the church should enable them to see that they have a vocation in the present, the vocation of being students up to the best of their ability, in preparation for the best exercise of their lifework later on. Perhaps one of the most effective ways in which the church might communicate this conviction would be through the general suspension of youth activities during examination periods, explicitly interpreted to the youth as being done in order that the church may affirm in actions as well as in words their primary calling as students. It is tragic to note how frequently a church's youth program will needlessly conflict with the scheduling of academic and extracurricular activities in the public schools. If it is true that the primary vocation of young students is to be students, then it is both unfair and self-defeating for the church in its scheduling to force young people needlessly into choices between school or church activities just because the church leaders have not taken the trouble to consult the school calendar. The way in which the church plans its youth program ought to communicate to youth the feeling that the church cares about the whole scope of their existence, particularly that rightfully dominant segment committed to the educational enterprise. The church should show its youth that it seeks to avoid conflicts with school functions whenever possible, not simply for the institution-centered goal of greater numerical success in its programming, but because it desires to affirm them in their pursuit of knowledge and skills.

Another way of communicating the same conviction would be to conduct what might be called a "homework retreat," even (or perhaps especially) around the time of examinations. The purpose of such a retreat would be to provide an opportunity to study for examinations and also to make an examination of why and how one studies. Many young people are not at all sure why they are studying or why they should study, and the reasons for studying that some of them hold may be sub-Christian ones centering on pride in grades or on desire for higher social and economic status as an end in itself. The proportion that would conceive of studying as their Christian calling as youth would surely be small. The anti-intellectualism, the cheating, the apathy or even dislike for their studies, and the pragmatic monomania for grades that in various degrees typify our young people are indications of an absence of any cogent sense of Christian vocation. A homework retreat affords an excellent setting for a Christian revaluation of the ultimate meaning of one's student years. Interspersed between periods of homework and recreational breaks, worship and discussion periods could communicate new insights concerning the relation between the Creator and the work of creation involved in schoolwork, between the quest for knowledge and God's intention that man come to the truth, and the relation between present study requirements and future occupational fitness.

This would also be a most appropriate setting in which youth might consider some of the central questions of their particular "vocational ethics," such as cheating, plagiarism, and the giving or receiving of unfair help, as well as such other matters as the value of various extracurricular activities in preparing for future usefulness and service and for leisure fulfillment. Of course, matters such as these can and should be the subject of program topics on other occasions as well; but the environment of a study retreat provides a context of especially fertile immediacy for significant conversation on the meaning of one's student years in the ultimate scheme of life. Those who have participated in retreats of this sort report that in addition to the meaningfulness of the dialogue, there is something quite inspiring even in the solitude of the homework periods. For in contrast with the atomistic *loneliness* of study in the impersonal atmosphere of a library, or in one's room, the corporate discipline of *solitude* in the midst of a silent but supportive community and fellowship concerned not only with learning but also with the ultimate reasons for learning forms part of an experience that can lead to renewed depth as well as vigor of commitment to the learning task.

Religion and the Arts

An emphasis within the church's program on literature and the other art forms can be an effective means of teaching people that the church recognizes God speaking and working in the world. Its attention to contemporary as well as classical drama and music and poetry, and even radio and television and movies, demonstrates that the church recognizes prophetic voices, largely outside the church, through whom God seeks to express his judgment and mercy for all men. Through its encouragement and hospitality toward these and other art forms as part of its teaching program, the church can help people understand the Christian imperative of willingness to look and listen with openness to what the artist is saying to our age and about our age, appealing to our powers of imagination as a means of heightening our awareness of aspects of modern life that we often see yet fail to observe to any significant degree.

A number of churches have taken notable strides in this direction by sponsoring exhibitions and concerts and performances on their own premises in connection with special programs. One form of this approach has been called a "festival of the arts," in which various media of artistic expression are successively presented in a series connected by one unifying theme that reflects in some way the relatedness between church and world. Such a festival, held on six successive Sunday evenings in Lent in one church and centering around the theme of "Broken Symbols in a Broken World," effectively employed exhibits of painting, photography, a choir concert, poetry readings, a recent French film, and a play by Bertolt Brecht to exhibit the employment of various artistic symbols to illustrate the brokenness of society, the alienation of man from man, and the reconciling action of God in Christ in breaking down dividing walls of conflict and alienation. In the case of this particular church, the Brecht drama was performed by a theatrical group made up of college students within the church. Professional drama groups, such as the Bishop's Company,[34] and semiprofessional groups connected with colleges and seminaries, can be imported for rather reasonable cost, as can outstanding foreign and domestic feature films.[35]

But admirable and valuable as such efforts may be, they are by no means the only way in which revelatory art forms can be integrated into a church's educational program. The church does not need to limit its exposure to art forms to the confines of the church building, nor does it need to arrange a special and rather self-consciously "arty" program series to communicate the fact that it takes seriously the secular proclamations of the arts. Various kinds of church groups can be encouraged to expose themselves to artistic enterprises in their normal secular locations. This can be done as an incidental means of enriching other lines of adult study rather than as a deliberate program emphasis in its own right.

In my own church, theater parties have been advantageously employed to supplement the reading and discussion of plays of theological significance, and even a couple of television performances that happened to fall on auspicious nights proved providentially suited to the current theme of group discussion. To synchronize such transient opportunities with the ongoing program development in church groups requires only a little imagination coupled with some modicum of advance information. Radio and television stations, theaters and playhouses, and the public relations offices of local colleges and universities are usually more than willing to provide any church or group that asks for it with advance information on lectures, exhibitions, film series, and other types of performances. Any alert and imaginative person on the church's education committee, such as a good audio-visual chairman, could suggest possible correlations between these offerings and the continuing program of various groups in the church. Such alertness and openness to the intellectual and aesthetic opportunities that the secular world provides can bear fruit not only in the instructive illustration of related religious themes of adult study but also through the encouragement it gives people to turn expectantly and perceptively to discover the revelatory activity of God in the secular world as well as in the church.

The Need to Experiment

Most of the suggestions contained in this chapter for helping to change the general stance of a parish outward toward its world do not necessarily call for the formation of new committees, new administrative tasks, or additional programs to be crammed into an already crowded parish calendar. For the most part, the suggestions offered here would be instead of, rather than in addition to, present ways of doing things. They are offered as new agenda for old committees, new themes and emphases in preaching and programming, new ways of conducting traditional activities. As such, these suggestions are essentially conservative, in the sense that their implementation would conserve and utilize whatever vitalities reside within present congregational structures and organizations.

If the New Testament analogy between the church and the human body is a truly viable and descriptive one, then church leaders should regard the total congeries of parish structure as an evolving organism with a history rather than as a mechanism that can be radically and abruptly altered on purely rational considerations, with no thought given to any organic trauma being thereby engendered. If the church is more aptly described as an organism than as a mechanism, then our passing of a verdict of irrelevance upon some particular organization or traditional activity should be followed by deliberations that consider subtler and less drastic forms of therapy before arriving at the conclusion that radical surgery or even amputation is indicated. As competent parish pathologists, it is important for us to find out why some organization or activity we regard as "sick" in terms of our understanding of the mission of the church continues to function at all, and what need, however apparently diseased, it still manages to fill. When these things are known, then changes can be implemented in such a way as to preserve whatever inherited parish structures are capable of renewal.

In many cases, we will not be able to answer this question until we make the attempt to inaugurate various changes, aimed at correcting the irrelevance and introversion from which some given aspect of the church's life is suffering. To shift the analogy slightly, we might say that we can only determine the strain-and-stress characteristics of old wineskins by pouring a little new wine into them. A business corporation can act in a far more cavalier and drastic fashion toward practices and departments that seem to be outmoded and unproductive in terms of the goals of the enterprise than can a church. Unlike a church, a corporation in many ways is more like a mechanism than an organic entity. Whether it is right that this be so is another matter. The point is that a corporation is far more able to excise the traditional to make room for the rational, to sweep away inept structures to make room for more efficient structures, than is the church.

But surely Daniel Jenkins is quite correct in insisting that the churches can and should expend at least as large a portion of their resources on research and experimentation as do our modern corporations, a portion that has increased in the past thirty years from 0.1 percent of our total national income then to 2 percent of a national income that is now four times larger.[36] The church, locally as well as denominationally, needs to mirror something of what Peter Drucker calls the "research explosion" of modern industry if it is to minister relevantly in a milieu of steadily accelerating social change. It must have the courage and the humble receptivity to devote more of its human and financial resources to tentative, experimental programs, perhaps similar to some of those suggested in this chapter, aimed at the renewal of mission within parish life. But lest the impulse for such renewal be strangled in intricate organizational entanglements, church leaders will reveal a spirit of wise respect for historical, organic continuities if they will channel their experimental ventures through inherited structures whenever possible before inaugurating new ones. A parish that would take seriously its particular mission will be characterized by a certain puritan austerity of structure, an economical simplicity in its institutional life that will avoid the self-defeating trap of creating new organizational complexes to sap the time and energies of both clergy and laity when the old forms might conceivably have been reshaped and utilized for the task.

The suggestions made in this chapter of ways in which the general orientation and posture of the laity may be turned outward toward the world are aimed at achieving simply that and no more. For the most part, they fall considerably short of what can and should be done in educating the laity for their ministry in the world. They are aimed at changing some of the motivations and attitudes of the laity, and such changes are only the preliminary groundwork for more specific learning. They can communicate a helpful Christian vocabulary, a needed definition of what the layman *is* within God's plan for the church, without being able in themselves to say much to him about what he is to *do* in the light of what in principle he *is*. A statement issued by the Department on the Laity of the World Council of Churches aptly describes our situation: "None of us fully understands, in our complex modern world, what this ministry of the laity really is. God reveals it to those who listen; every situation in His world can speak to us." Orienting a parish outward toward the world enables it to listen, to hear God speaking in the revelatory character of every specific situation each layman faces. It also can arouse some lay people to seek specific guidance within the offerings of the educational program of the church. In the next two chapters we shall consider the nature and the varieties of special group opportunities the local church might provide to meet this need.

Chapter V

The Role of Concern Groups

THE CHURCH in its local expression needs to devise a structure and machinery whereby the congregation is broken down into natural and indigenous groups that at the same time promote the pastoral care and training of the laity, and produce working groups for the simultaneous expansion of the Church within large amorphous populations."[37] This statement by E. R. Wickham in *Church and People in an Industrial Society* is expressive of a strong consensus among those concerned for the renewal of the church in its ministry to the world. A growing number of churchmen are coming to the conclusion that weekly services and large organizational gatherings in the church building simply are not enough to enable the members of a congregation, widely dispersed throughout the world during most of the week, to experience the reality of their collective identity as members of the body of Christ. Many would even agree with Bishop John A. T. Robinson's assertion that a cellular structure, in which the church is formed as a sort of honeycomb of small units rather than as an amorphous aggregation of people, is an absolute necessity for the church's existence.[38]

One dimension of expression for this concern for cell group structuring is to be seen in the development of the house church or neighborhood or zone group. This residentially based type of grouping is a relevant matrix for training the laity for more effective Christian servanthood in family life and local community affairs. Many of those who have experimented with this form of concern group have found it a far more effective means of touching people's daily life in households and neighborhoods than programs geographically centered in a church building. The latter suffer from the fact that very frequently the geographical distances separating the home and neighborhood setting of the various participants leads to psychological distance in the life of the group.

The neighborhood group has the additional advantage of making the presence of the church a bit more visible in the residential midst of the unchurched, and thereby provides new opportunities for meaningful encounter by including them in such a natural gathering. Experience has shown that persons will often find their way into the church fellowship through a "neighborhood congregation," after the failure of many efforts to get them to begin by coming to functions at the church building. The formation of cells on the basis of residence also can perform the important Christian service of helping to create a viable community structure, creating and strengthening lines of communication in neighborhood networks all around the parish where previously little or no true community might have existed. Furthermore, concern groups for the improvement of the laity's ministry as parents probably would gain more than they would lose if they were structured along neighborhood rather than along age-group lines. A regional community of interest and neighborhood friendship might prove to be a more cohesive and significant bond than a community of interest based upon the coincidences of children's ages within the larger parish area.

Another meaningful basis for the structuring of Christian cells or concern groups is to convene them by occupational categories. The structuring of Christian concern groups along occupational lines has the virtue of following natural forces of social cohesion that are at least as strong as those of residential identity. Many observers of our social scene maintain that human community, in our modern industrial and commercial world, is no longer primarily a matter of geographical relationship within a residential neighborhood but, rather, a central fact of professional and vocational life. The community that exists among co-workers is for many a more inclusive and formative frame of reference than any number of associational connections with one's neighbors during the hours away from work. Whether geographically centralized in plant or store, or geographically diffused as in the case of professional associations, these clearly identifiable communities constitute almost virgin territory for the church's educational mission.

A Christian concern group, whether it be centered in the community of residence or the community of work, the place of consumption or the place of production, is a community within a community, a part that seeks to minister to a larger whole through the Christian nurture it brings to its members. One of its purposes should be to seek to heighten its members' Christian awareness of just who they are, that they are lay ministers, each of whom has been given through the specifics of his life situation a little "congregation" of fellow workers, friends, family, and neighbors to be served. It should also sharpen their perception and awareness of what is really going on in the midst of all that is apparently going on in the involvements and responsibilities of these communities of work and residence, especially as this includes a theological perception of God's providential activity in our collective life.

To be sure, the discovery of the meaning and most suitable shape of one's lay ministry in his daily work is essentially a lonely, solitary task, because only the individual can fully grasp all the unique specifics of the concrete situation in which he is called to minister. No concern group can lead one by the hand every step of the way. Nevertheless, one of the vital functions of such a group is to help make this difficult task a little easier through the sharing of insights and experiences from which one may profit, and by the supportive recognition this brings that there are others who are making conscientious attempts to exercise a Christian ministry themselves in the same general kind of secular situation, that there are others who share this concern. The imparting of this kind of vocational guidance, which can be accomplished with more effective specificity through fairly specialized occupational groups than through the parish church as a whole, is surely one of the most important ministries that a church can provide to strengthen in turn the ministry of its members. For the church itself is called into existence by God, and the specific calling of each Christian is mediated to him through the fellowship and communication of the church; and a person's sense of calling is made more specific and relevant, and receives more meaningful collective support, in smaller and more specialized groups.

John A. T. Robinson points to this need for specificity of meaning and purpose in one's sense of Christian calling:

> Religion may offer a man a place and purpose in the ultimate scheme of things, but he is not likely to be remotely interested in it, unless he can see it as giving him in the first instance a place and a purpose in the immediate setting in which he lives. It is when he sees the Gospel discovering to him social salvation, that is, a position in society in which he really finds himself, where he counts, is of value, and can make a difference, that a man may begin to understand a gospel promising him "right standing" with God.[39]

It is within the context of the small Christian cell, focusing on the specific meanings in one's daily work, that a person can most easily find that highly concrete sense of self-identity under God without which questions of more ultimate meaning may seem rather academic. And the question of meaning—the ability to answer the question, Who am I?—precedes the ethical or tactical question of, What am I to do? as my Christian obedience in response to my providentially given vocational identity. The individual is perhaps even more dependent upon a small group experience for the answer to this logically and experientially prior question of theological self-identity than he is for answers to consequent questions of ethics and policy in his occupation. The high degree of technical specialization and particularity involved in most occupational decision-making situations makes ethical generalizations both difficult to arrive at and of somewhat limited value, whereas a group consensus of conviction concerning the general Christian meaning of vocational responsibilities and opportunities can be of great significance to group members despite rather considerable differences of detail in their respective jobs.

The process of communication is quite obviously of the very essence of the life of a Christian cell centered around a vocational concern, and facilitating the improvement of communication within the community of work is surely one of the most noteworthy Christian services that a cell group can perform, not only for its own immediate membership, but also for those others with whom group members may come in contact in the course of their daily work. Among fellow workers there very frequently exists a quite considerable amount of talk about matters of mutual concern related to their immediate work objectives, but usually this talk is purely technical shoptalk, or perhaps it is little more than a trading of platitudes and shibboleths uncritically reflecting the approved cant and accepted ideology of the professional, commercial, or industrial ingroup to which they belong. In the course of their life at work people seldom have the opportunity to come together to talk about the human problems inherent in their work situations in an atmosphere of freedom. Vocational cell groups are eminently suited by their very nature for the fostering of such vitally needed communication. They constitute a humanizing influence upon those who directly participate in them and upon those who come in touch with these participants, thus helping to counteract the dehumanizing obstruction of communication that seems to characterize much of modern work life. And surely whatever serves to make human life more truly human serves the purposes of One who sent his Son as perfect Man that our own humanity might be restored and redeemed through him.

The church is of immense value as servant to the world in simply providing opportunities for reflective thinking and the exchange of significant ideas and feelings, inasmuch as this kind of vital conversation is so often crowded out both at work and at home by daily crises and deadlines, and by escapist small talk that skirts encounters with life's deeper issues. In forming concern cells the church is fostering the kind of serious two-way conversation that ought to be occurring around the family table, the company lunchroom table, and in political and civic groups of various sorts, but which unfortunately is often woefully lacking.

Franklin Littell illustrates the fruits of this kind of ministry to the world on the part of the Christian church as he describes the impact of the lay academies on the quality of postwar German life. He cites evidence to the effect that all over Germany there are economic and political groups using democratic methods of discussion and decision-making that were first learned in sessions at the lay academies. The experience of key persons from all walks of life in small groups at the academies has functioned as a leavening influence in the group life of unions, political parties, and professional organizations, with open-ended discussions taking the place of the rigid polarization of sophist debate, and a concern for group consensus and democratic interpersonal relations replacing some of the ironfisted authoritarianism that had totally characterized German social life.[40]

The Christian church is fulfilling a part of its intended servant role whenever it provides training in group life that improves the functioning of human society, whenever it helps to counteract some of the demonic distortions of interpersonal relationships that curb human creativity and personal growth. Whatever facilitates serious communication between husbands and wives, between neighbors, between superiors and subordinates at work, creating an atmosphere of receptivity to criticism and to the suggestion of alternative proposals and the interjection of new ideas, makes human life more human and so serves God's purposes for our collective existence.

The Case Study Method

In a 1956 consultation at the Ecumenical Institute at Bossey concerning the training of the laity for their ministry in the world, the summary report declared that the facilitation of communication through training in the art of dialogue and imaginative perception into social situations was of central importance in preparing the laity for a ministry of reconciliation in secular life. It would be quite difficult to take intelligent exception to this conclusion. If the ministry of the laity is a ministry of reconciliation between man and man as well as between God and man, then surely proficiency in two-way communication should be a crucial part of lay training, and probably no more suitable matrix for such training exists than in the small vocational cell group. Group experience provides the most relevant training ground for effective witness in a world in which the area determined by individual decisions is narrowing, while that determined by group decisions is expanding. Christian obedience that is causally significant in such a world must increasingly consist of endeavors to communicate persuasively so as to influence the decisions of one's group—whether that group be a board of directors, a union committee, a party precinct gathering, or whatever—to conform most nearly to what one believes to be God's purpose for collective human life.

Training in the skills of dialogue and acuity of social perception, skills that are of vital significance in meaningful communication, by their very nature require a group context for their exercise and development. More specifically it can be said that the case study method within a group situation provides perhaps the most realistic setting for such training. The case study method may be defined as the presentation of actual or at least realistically hypothetical situations or episodes of "cases" to serve as a basis for group discussion. Case studies may be presented as read or narrated reports, as audio-visual presentations of a specific problem, or even in the form of sociodrama or role-play. The case study, particularly when presented in a role-play form, can be helpful in developing the group's skill in dialogue by subjecting the group to the discipline of constructing a line of conversation appropriate to a concrete situation that symbolizes a common and acknowledged obstacle to dialogue in daily life, guiding the group into an active conversation with the situation. The case study method is also helpful, again especially when the case in question is role-played, in developing skills in imaginative and empathetic perception. It gives the participants practice in projecting themselves into the emotional and intellectual world of others, and then seeing a little more objectively their own reactions thereto.

Educational experience may be conceptualized in terms of a cycle consisting of *thought* leading to *words* leading to *deeds*, leading in turn to new retrospective thoughts and a repetition of the cycle. Oftentimes group discussion will be characterized by abstract, generalized thought leading to abstract, generalized words, and never issuing in any particular deeds at all because of the high level of abstraction in the discussion. Beginning with abstractions based on Biblical theology, a group thus may move on to exchanges of theologically correct words, but never complete the cycle through a discovery of the relevance of these abstract words to concrete deeds in life.

The use of the case study method allows a group to come in on this thought-word-deed cycle at its most concrete and life-centered point, starting with the real or hypothetical deed represented by the case in question. Moving from consideration of the specific deed, a group then may turn to the content of Christian thought, armed with pointed and meaningfully concrete questions. Since ethics is preeminently concerned with deeds, the case study technique is particularly helpful for getting at the root of ethical questions. The introduction of a case study often comes as a relief to a group, especially after it has been floundering for a time at a more abstract level of discussion, providing a situation with which participants can identify and thereby restoring a sense of reality to the discussion. Then, after a case has been presented and considered, the subsequent discussion of deeper underlying issues and general ethical directives and axioms is much more vital by virtue of its relation to a common base of experience. The Department of the Church and Economic Life of the National Council of Churches wisely recognized the particular suitability of this type of approach in the prospectus it prepared for its experimental Pilot Occupational Ethics Project, which urged the use of case studies as a method. But although the case study method is especially well suited to discussions centering around the ethical aspects of the layman's ministry, as the linguistic relatedness of the words "case" and "casuistry" suggests, the method is also helpful in opening up discussions on such other matters as policy-making and human relations in a far broader sense than the purely ethical.

As has been implied, there is no reason why cases presented need be factual, even in part, provided that fictitious cases are composed by someone fully involved in that aspect of secular life in the world which happens to be the group's common denominator and who is therefore knowledgeable concerning what is necessary to make a case ring true for a group. Indeed, a hypothetical or heavily disguised case may be the only way of enabling a group to deal with an issue without violating confidences or indulging in scapegoating, or jeopardizing some person's job relationships. But whether actual or hypothetical, experience has shown that the case presented should be understandable to group participants without requiring endless elaboration of unfamiliar detail in the presentation, although all essential details should be known at least to the proposer of the case, and preferably to the group as well, when a factual case is involved.

Let the World Write the Agenda

To the extent that case studies are utilized to structure a Christian concern group's meetings, the world is indeed "writing the agenda" for the group. Of course, this may be the situation in a group even when the case study method is not used, especially if the literature about work, or leisure, or family life or politics, or whatever other concern the group is pursuing is not explicitly and verbally Christian in its language or even in its point of view, and if in addition the group discussion does not introduce such language. The absence of patently identifiable religious language doubtless would be upsetting to many, accustomed as they are to identifying the gathered life of the Christian community with the use of a special Christian vocabulary. The conviction is often deep-rooted in the lay mind that the employment of a peculiar language is inseparably annexed to the assembly of the "peculiar people" (I Peter 2:9, KJV) of God. Yet the experience of a number of industrial mission staff people and other theologically trained participants in vocational concern groups indicates that much of our traditional Christian vocabulary strikes virtually no responsive chord among lay people, at least not with regard to any perceived relevance to their occupational involvements. Terms and phrases such as sin, justification by faith, vocation as special calling from God, and human creativity as part of the divine ordinance and plan for man to "fill the earth and subdue it," may perhaps be seen as meaningful with regard to the narrowly private and familial sectors of daily life, but people seem to have difficulty perceiving the applicability of such terminology to the more public sector of their human involvements. Evidently the traditional formulations of the truth of the gospel stand in need of revision or restatement, in need of translation into terms and structures of thought that are meaningful in the context of modern work life.

The relationship between a clergyman or other religious professional as theological resource person and the laymen in a vocational group is somewhat analogous to that which exists between a professional missionary and those who are "native" to a particular culture or subculture with its particular language and world view. In both situations, the task of effective translation is essential to the task of mission, and it requires a two-way process of communication and mutual understanding of the meanings in the local "dialect" which can be correlated with the meanings in the universal gospel. Neither in the one case nor in the other can the professional churchman do all the work of translation by himself, no matter how strenuously he may study the local language and customs, no matter how long or how carefully he may listen for local inflections and nuances of meaning. The laity themselves have to discover correlations of meaning between Christian affirmations and their daily experience in the world if the process of translation is to result in effective communication; and it would seem that this kind of communication is more likely to take place in a situation in which daily life is examined in the light of Christian affirmations rather than the other way around. In the more traditional situation of course, the data of secular experience is used, if at all, simply as an illustrative appendage to a course in Bible study or some other form of technical theological verbalizing.

By letting life in the world write the agenda, so to speak, instead of using it didactically to illustrate some theological point, we allow real life to raise the questions, and to raise them in terms the world understands, so that the verbalization of Christian answers has to be made as a disciplined response required by the nature of the empirical situation being examined. Therefore, the literature used by a vocational group or any other kind of special concern group for that matter, as its primary stimulus to thinking and discussion, can quite properly be thoroughly secular, in the sense of being devoid of explicitly Christian vocabulary or concepts. The formation of a concern group need not depend on whether or not some denominational or interdenominational publishing house has produced a discussion manual neatly outlining a study course structure for the particular occupational category or other special concern to be represented in the group. Indeed, a group would probably function much better without such a crutch, except perhaps one written by a lay person of special competence in theology as well as in his line of work or other secular responsibility under discussion.

It should be obvious that giving a strongly secular orientation to the content of a group's reading and discussion need not at all imply an abandonment of theological concern. Surely the course of a group's discussion can be profoundly theological without being explicitly centered upon the Bible or other explicit theological language, if it is dealing with ultimate questions about the meaning of that segment of worldly existence around which the group has been convened. Theological reflection can fairly and appropriately be defined as the opening up of the data of human experience to an examination of the deeper dimensions of its meaning, both proximate and ultimate, and a consideration of one's self-identity in terms of present expectations, future goals and plans, and ultimate commitments. Such reflection can be carried on without any self-conscious dependence upon traditional theological terminology. As Bishop Wickham, the pioneer in the field of industrial mission work, has reminded us, the training of the laity is not totally encompassed in the mere imparting of theological instruction. "Its essence," he declares, "is the wrestling of men in the same secular situations with their own problems in the light of common basic insights deduced from their faith."[41] If God is, in Bonhoeffer's words, "the 'beyond' in the midst of life, . . . not on the borders of life but at its center," then surely a group is involved in a significant theological enterprise seeking to discern the workings of God, and man's appropriate response to God's activity, whenever it is probing realistically into any significant aspect of human existence, whether or not technical theological language is employed.

Obviously, such grappling with secular problems in the light of the faith presupposes at least some modicum of theological literacy within the group. It is a tragic fact that usually the church has imparted theological instruction in utter abstraction from life in the world. The secular context and language of a concern group constitutes a challenge to the group's theological resource person to furnish the explicitly theological information and insights that are directly appropriate to various specific points in the secular dialogue. Such explicit theological information thus is presented in the form of tentative answers, or perhaps counterquestions, to questions or problems posed in secular terminology by the group. As the group evaluates this information, testing its relevance and perhaps seeking to translate it into terms that are more familiar and comprehensible in their common secular situation, there is a process of creative dialogue not only between persons but also between two often isolated aspects of personal experience and commitment, between specific life problems and generalized theological convictions.

This kind of dialogic alternation between theological reflection and life in the world serves the integrative function of bringing people together at a point where two focuses of their concern coalesce—their common faith and their common concern in the world, whether that concern be neighborhood matters, their family life, their occupation, or some particular social issue. The dialogue in the group becomes the vital point of intersection between the vertical personal dimension of theological commitment and the horizontal social dimension of commitments in the world. In the context of such a dialogue, the introduction of data concerning Biblical theology becomes stimulus material for helping people to discover the meaning of their own history and their own decisions in history, in reflection on the meaning of Biblical history, and especially helping them to see the essential congruence between the Biblical perception of the divine activity in political, economic, and social events of Biblical times and the perception of that activity in their own social existence.

The trouble with much that passes for Biblical and doctrinal study among lay people is that very often this material is studied and examined in a deductive, abstract propositional form that takes no cognizance of the antecedent human questions and needs for which the body of Christian doctrine is intended to provide answers. An unashamedly secular orientation in the dialogue of a Christian concern group allows the world to write the agenda by posing its own authentic questions in its own way and in its own terms so that technical theological affirmations of ultimate meaning are perceived as the background dimension of divine depth behind the examination of the more immediate and evident meaning of any human situation and the responses for which it seems to call.

Chapter VI

Family Life Education

A CONSIDERABLE PORTION of the laity's time, in its dispersion in the world, is spent in family life. The ministry of husbands and wives to one another, and of both to their children, is a very important part of the ministry of the laity in the world. Within the circle of family relationships they may participate in the work of God in the world and be engaged in the ministry of the church in the world. Thus family life is a vocation, and a church concerned for the ministry of its people should provide educational opportunities for the more adequate exercise of this vocation even if it provides for no other. The formation of parent education groups deserves high priority in the education of the laity for their ministry for a number of reasons.

One of the most obvious reasons is the fact that family life is the largest single vocational common denominator in a congregation. Whatever the diversity of their other ministries, the vast majority live in families. As husband and wife seek to meet one another's physical and emotional needs, and the corresponding needs of their children, they are performing a part of the role of servanthood that is their calling. Family life education has a further advantage as a starting point in the fact that the strong family orientation already inherent in the typical parish structure and program provides a ready matrix for this particular area of lay training which requires only a fairly minimal degree of restructuring and organizational innovation. Training in aspects of Christian responsibility in family life can with relative ease be integrated into the program pattern of existing parish organizations such as couples clubs, women's associations and circles, and youth organizations. The increasing prevalence of such special noncontinuing structures as church family night programs and workshops and summer family camping also constitutes a series of ready-made opportunities for this emphasis. Furthermore, the family is the one area of responsibility in the world for which a sizable number of people in the churches already recognize their need for help. The United Presbyterian Church's survey of families revealed a widespread desire for family life education through parents groups, despite the common complaint against the local church's overorganization and frantic hyperactivity in other dimensions of its institutional life. The interviews uncovered a real hunger for the kind of personal association in groups where issues that really matter in family life could be explored.

Still another reason for starting with Christian family life groups is the fact that amid the complexity and impersonality of most of the roles that adults are called upon to fulfill in modern society, the circle of family relationships stands out as being perhaps the least complex and most personal of all. Adults in the church will often come to parents discussion groups for almost purely pragmatic reasons, for help with specific problems, not initially thinking of their parental role as a form of ministry. If such groups can enable them to see their various familial roles as ministries, they will be in a better position to realize their ministerial calling in more complex and less intimately personal situations in their world.

The generally pragmatic and sub-Christian orientation of parents in their initial interest in parents discussion groups in the church was evident in the findings of the Presbyterian family survey. The researchers found ample evidence that the majority of parents in the survey had not grasped even the most basic affirmations of the Christian faith, and therefore were unable to think theologically about their life together as families. They seldom evaluated their family activities in terms of the Christian faith instead of by some other standard. The parents were asked what kind of family experiences they most wanted their children to remember in later years. The great majority of the parents (86.2 percent) wanted their children to remember above all else the loving, happy relationships within the family, relationships characterized by helpfulness, sympathy, and respect. Only a small minority of the parents (17 percent) wanted their children to remember most of all the Christian faith that unified the family, an awareness of God's guidance and love, or service to persons outside the family.[42]

This survey would seem to have a number of important implications for the nature of Christian family life education in the church. It seems to point to a need for discussion groups in which parents may be led to grasp some of the theological implications in their family relationships. The researchers detected among the parents a far better understanding of psychology than of theology. The recorded interviews are dotted with psychological jargon, much of it employed in a knowledgeable way. By comparison, theological terminology and theologically informed insights in secular terminology were scarce. This situation would seem to call for an approach that would examine specific problems in family living from a quite explicitly and even didactically Biblical and doctrinal viewpoint, especially the important correlations between psychological and theological insights, in order to enable parents to begin to think theologically about their family life as a whole. Parents are often at a loss to engage in meaningful conversation with their children about such basic matters as sexual standards or the meaning of death, to cite two examples, primarily because of their theological illiteracy. These parents need to be given a theological conception of sex, of death, of discipline, and of other such matters of importance to their ministry.

The Problem of Leisure

Along with the other theological conceptions that parents need, they need a theology of leisure. In a pragmatic, untheological way, they seem to be aware of this need themselves. The parents in the Presbyterian survey were asked to list on a questionnaire those items which they saw as a family problem needing some solution during the preceding year. The first on the list in order of frequency was the problem of television and radio listening and viewing, and in third place was the question of recreation and leisure-time practices. With the five-day, forty-hour workweek presently regarded as normative, and with the real possibility of its being even further shortened, together with the labor-saving conveniences in the modern home, the increasing availability of free time that a family can use as it chooses is becoming a major problem in American culture. Furthermore, approximately 15 percent of total consumer expenditures are currently spent on leisure-time activities. The creative stewardship of our ever-increasing wealth in discretionary time and discretionary dollars requires careful thought of the kind that can come from the collective wisdom of a group of people who are aware of the theological significance of leisure. A family's discretionary time and money can be molded into a significant instrument of ministry when activities are planned that help the family in educational, cultural, and physical development for the sake of ministry to one another and to others as well.

Prominent social observers have been pointing to the growing importance of the family unit, and more particularly the physical home location itself, as the primary locus of leisure activity in our culture, not to mention its significance as a learning center imparting very influential guidance concerning patterns of consumption and free-time social participation. Consequently, the church's program of family life education, and more particularly various forms of parent education, would seem to be the most strategic point for considering the whole problem of leisure. In essence, Christian education for leisure is an aspect of stewardship education, especially the stewardship one is to exercise with regard to his free time. Like other forms of stewardship education, it is education in values, education in making choices between various modes and avenues of expenditure, with one's time off from his major occupation being the chief commodity in question.

Robert Lee, Sebastian de Grazia, and others have recently been reminding us of how imprecise we have been in the use of the word "leisure." We have indiscriminately applied it to all of one's time off, whereas both classical philosophy and the Christian tradition have distinguished carefully between merely "killing" or filling or passing time and using it creatively, applying the term "leisure" only to its creative use. A Christian stewardship of free time that will transform it into true "leisure" involves making choices that use time for creative ends, for the furtherance of such values as deepening and enlarging one's understanding of himself and his world, for recreating his body and mind, for strengthening the bonds of community with friends and kindred. In terms of such a definition of leisure, it is obvious that the utilization of free time by a considerable majority of the people in the churches is so mawkish and trivial as to be scarcely deserving of the term "leisure."

Therefore one of the chief aims of the program of adult education should be the nurturing of a Christian discrimination and taste, the development of basic canons of judgment for making truly creative choices amid the plethora of options for the expenditure of discretionary time and money offered by our increasingly consumer-oriented culture. This scarcely needs to take the form of providing music or art appreciation courses, hobby clubs, lists of recommended movies and television shows, or similar paraphernalia. Such specific aids to intelligent discrimination are readily accessible quite outside the institutional structures of the church, and they are usually handled in a far more competent fashion than the church could reasonably hope to achieve within the limitations of its institutional resources. Therefore, family life education should have as one of its objectives the motivation of parents to seek out such guides to judgment as an expression of an underlying commitment to more creative employment of the family's time together. Because of the general adequacy of many of these secular resources, the church need not provide a great deal of specific "consumer education"; however, it should communicate to people an attitude toward life that will prompt them to seek out competent consumer guidance as a means of grace in this important aspect of their life. The church should help men and women to see that they are called not only as workers and homemakers, not only as producers, but also as consumers, that they are as responsible to God for their leisure as they are for their daily work.

In order to help people to perceive this, the church is going to have to rethink its entire theology of leisure. Traditionally, when the teaching and preaching of the church has had anything at all to say about leisure, it has usually spoken of leisure's significance as being somehow ancillary and subsidiary to one's daily work. It has usually conceived of leisure's value as being functional and instrumental rather than as an intrinsic good in itself, defining leisure as "recreation" in the narrow sense of its utility for re-creating and restoring the individual's various powers for the sake of his central occupation. This totally work-oriented estimation of the significance of leisure is exemplified in a study book on the meaning of Christian vocation written for laymen under the auspices of the Presbyterian Church U.S. Its author, Wade H. Boggs, Jr., enunciates the typical Calvinist viewpoint which still seems to predominate whenever the church addresses its people on the subject of leisure:

> Finally, the weekly Sabbath patterned after the example of the Creator *has no meaning apart from* the background of six days of *labor*. The Sabbath of rest provides for that rhythm of rest and work and worship which is *essential to the continued efficiency of labor* (italics mine).[43]

This kind of moralizing obscures the full scope of the doctrine of the calling of every Christian, the fact that every Christian has a calling, a vocation, not merely in a narrowly occupational sense, but more broadly a calling to an all-inclusive way of life that includes all his hours and recognizes an *intrinsic* value in each of them. Discussions of criteria for family leisure activities need to dispel this merely recuperative, occupation-oriented appraisal of it, instilling instead a point of view that affirms personal fulfillment and self-understanding as legitimate goals in the Christian's use of leisure time, quite apart from whatever utility it may or may not have as refreshment for work time. Such an approach need in no way become a justification for a purely egoistic "fun morality" that is inimical to any real sense of social responsibility beyond the narrow confines of the family unit. For genuine leisure not only has a recuperative and re-creative function in relation to one's occupation, and a creative and therapeutic function in relation to one's need for constructive self-love; it also has an altruistic function in the expression of neighbor-love through political and civic involvements.

Thus politics and various forms of community service surely constitute an important aspect of a Christian conception of leisure as the constructive utilization of free time, though there the goal is not primarily that of re-creation for the individual; moreover, no study of the family members' stewardship in the utilization of their free time should fail to consider them as such. Indeed, whatever efforts a church makes to encourage and educate its people for civic and political responsibilities, whether in connection with parent education or in other contexts, may be said to constitute Christian education for stewardship through leisure.

The inclusion of considerations concerning the utilization of free time for meaningful leisure in the curriculum of family life education can take either of two basic forms. Either it can be approached directly as an explicitly defined problem for study and discussion or it can be indirectly incorporated into a primary emphasis on family consumer responsibilities, or into some other broad aspect of family interrelations of which family lesiure choices are quite clearly an integral part. In the former case, use can be made of some of the material in the rapidly growing body of literature on the subject of leisure, for a direct and explicit frontal attack on this increasingly pressing problem. But whether or not a group of parents chooses to identify family-time utilization as a specific problem for topical consideration in and of itself, no curriculum of parent education can be said to be complete unless either directly or indirectly the leisure question comes into consideration. The Presbyterian family survey would seem to indicate that many parents are likely to desire a self-conscious and direct approach to the question of leisure in family life. However, the absence in any given group of an evident desire to take a head-on approach to the meaning of leisure and various family leisure options should not be construed as indicating that leisure does not constitute a significant issue for the members of the group to deal with, perhaps in some less self-conscious manner.

The Feminine Role

While consideration of the leisure question is important and desirable in any program of parent education, it is particularly pertinent and appropriate in groups of mothers alone. It does little good for church leaders to bewail the unfortunate fact that for every couple concerned enough to participate in opportunities for parent education there is probably another mother or two who for various reasons would have to participate without her husband and who would like to do so. All the moralistic expostulating and scolding in the world will not alter the fact that in our present culture fatherhood is perceived as an avocation at best, in contrast with the generally acknowledged status of motherhood as a full vocation, at least for one period in a woman's life. Instead of wringing their hands over the alleged abdication of the role of responsible fatherhood in our culture, church program planners should put their hands to the task of providing opportunities for women to gather in groups for mutual assistance and support in fulfilling their common vocational responsibility as mothers.

Such groups of women can bear a particularly significant relationship to the whole question of Christian stewardship of leisure because of the extent to which wives and mothers shape and determine the family's utilization of its time together. They are to a large extent the "bearers of the ethos," the shapers and transmitters of cultural patterns and values, the arbiters of taste who largely control and channel family expenditures of time and money. The books, the magazines, the television programs, the neighborhood involvements to which her family shall be exposed is very largely in the woman's hands. A family's evening and weekend activities, and their educational and cultural content, are generally shaped to a very considerable extent by her. Even the general character of the residential community, in which as Sebastian de Grazia reminds us free time still is largely spent, depends in large measure on the use she has made of her own leisure in creating a fabric of communication and relationship in the community, both along formal organizational lines and also along the lines of informal friendship ties. The transformation of a cluster of dwelling units into a viable neighborhood structure, and the maintenance of such a structure in the face of rapid population mobility, is largely the work of those adults who spend the greatest portion of their waking hours there, the wives and mothers who establish a network of formal and informal communication that in considerable measure determines the social climate. With such vast formative powers in their hands for determining which values shall prevail in our use of free time, education in Christian values concerning the uses of leisure is deserving of a high priority of concern within the total women's program of the church. Women seem to need to be helped to become aware of the actual extent of their dominance in the formation of patterns of leisure, and beyond this, to perceive the exercise of their powerful influence in shaping leisure life as a vital part of their particular ministry in the world.

Feminine influence in family life is of course weighty in many other matters besides leisure choices. Women's choices are largely determinative not only of leisure choices, but also of family dollar expenditures, 80 percent of which they manage directly. They hold title to 40 percent of the nation's homes, they are the beneficiaries of two thirds of all life insurance policies, and they constitute 43 percent of all stockholders. And when we add to all this the dominance of women in every aspect of the rearing of children, including whatever degree or kind of religious nurture is given in the home, it becomes increasingly obvious that a program of family life education that is primarily centered around couples in the church, effectually excluding many women whose husbands are uninterested or unable to participate in such a program because of scheduling during evening hours, is severely self-limited in its leavening influence. Quite possibly a good program of Christian family life education can have as one of its beneficent results a partial redress of the wide imbalance that typically exists between the respective roles of husbands and wives in child-rearing, and in the shaping of family life in general. Such modifications of the presently prevalent pattern in the direction of fuller parental partnership constitute laudable and reasonable goals, and they are most likely to be achieved when husbands themselves are willing and able to participate in the program of parent education. Still, the fact remains that the scope of the woman's responsibility for family life is inevitably greater than her husband's. Thus, even beyond the Christian education they both need for this shared ministry in the home, and which the husband may be quite willing and conscientiously committed to receive, women need the opportunity to come together to share insights and to support one another in family responsibilities that are perforce more detailed and more inclusive of their total existence and its Christian meaning than is ever to be the case with their husbands.

There are a host of pressing issues of Christian concern to women as wives and mothers that are not faced by husbands and fathers, or at least not in the same way. The social ascendancy of the career woman in our day, the glamorization of her role in the romanticizing of work outside the home, tend to make motherhood and homemaking seem rather insignificant and tedious by comparison, depriving the homemaker of the satisfaction of the recognized and revered status that in former days undergirded her self-identity. The popularity of many modern books and magazine articles on the changing feminine role points to a present crisis of meaning in the self-understanding of multitudes of women. The general tone of this literature tends to be rebellious with regard to women's domestic responsibilities. Instead of pointing to sources of meaning and satisfaction intrinsic to these responsibilities, this literature proposes the general solution of escape into outside employment at the earliest feasible moment. It largely dismisses the option of community service through volunteer work as being dreary and mindless busywork for the most part, although it fails to make clear why receiving a paycheck should make a job intrinsically more meaningful and satisfying. Nevertheless, the popularity of this literature of the continuing feminine revolution, in sharp contrast with the vapid sentimentalizing of motherhood that generally characterized a previous social epoch, indicates the extent of the crisis in vocational self-identity among multitudes of modern women.

In response to the deep need present in this vocational crisis, it is the responsibility of the church to convene groups of women, not only for discussions on Christian education in the home and child-rearing in general, but also to talk about themselves: how they feel about their present and perspective roles, and what light the Christian message casts upon their self-understanding. Behind their mission as churchwomen, or as agents of Christian education in the home, and behind any interest they may have in learning about the institutional mission activities of the church, lies the psychologically and theologically prior question of their own mission as homemakers, and especially of their attitudes toward this mission and vocation. The mass media are already sharply aware of how keenly interested women are in the examination of the feminine role. When will the church finally respond and initiate structures for dialogue on this issue within a context of basic Christian affirmations concerning the significance of every social role? With some of the current literature of feminine unrest used as a foil for dialogue at one extreme, and reminiscences of the sentimentalizing Mother's Day cant of a bygone day at the other, groups of women can work over that fertile middle ground between an unchristian demeaning of the domestic role and an equally unchristian idealizing or absolutizing of it. The convening of such concern groups among women in the church can follow neighborhood or age lines or some other natural or even purely arbitrary demarcation. However, it probably should *not* follow the age lines of children in the family, not only because of the inevitable overlapping, but also because the purpose of the group should be to examine the total constellation of feminine roles, not simply the role of child-rearing.

The working woman faces a situation that in many ways is quite unique. With approximately one third of all women working outside the home, almost any church would have enough working women in its membership sufficiently concerned about some of the human problems involved in filling two nearly full-time roles to form a group dealing with the special problems this presents.

Another interesting possibility would be to convene a group of couples, or perhaps just wives if necessary, around the common concern of dependence on one large corporation for their income, their geographical and social mobility, the amount and spacing of time when they can be together, and other factors influencing the quality of family life. "Corporation wives" and corporation families, because of the extent to which corporation affairs impinge on all their domestic arrangements, share a most significant common denominator of interest regardless of the varieties of job function and of levels in the corporation hierarchy that may be represented among the breadwinners in any given church. Often there will be in one church a sufficient concentration of people connected with the same company to make this highly feasible as a basis for convening one or more Christian family life groups. But regardless of the basis upon which such groups are gathered, the area of the husband's work life, and all the sociocultural factors it introduces into family life, belongs within a truly adequate curriculum for family life education.

One significant danger to be avoided in the church's program of family life education is that of fostering an idolatry centering on the family. Just as the local church itself is prone to an idolatrous introversion upon its own institutional concerns, so the family also is prone to see itself as an institution within which each member should be able to find complete fulfillment for the meaning of his life. The Presbyterian survey found church families to be almost completely child-centered in their orientation. "Parent-child relations" headed the list of suggestions given by parents, and the list given by pastors too, regarding possible topics for family life education. In the group interviews, the parents' fear of in any way alienating their children appeared with surprising regularity in the discussion of discipline problems. The researchers declared that the parents in the survey tended to be preoccupied with their children to the point of virtually eliminating any significant personal life for the adults. One important aspect of adult life that was all but crowded out by all the child-centered discussion in the interviews was the relation between the husband's work and his family life.[44] There was little serious discussion about the ethical dilemmas faced by the breadwinner in his employment, and there was a lack of insight into the relationships between occupational values and family living. A husband's occupation is a fundamental determinant of a family's entire situation. It often dictates where they live, who their friends are, what their recreation will be, and how their children are reared. Yet the discussions in the group interviews revealed no awareness of the influence of the breadwinner's occupation on family values and patterns of living. This tendency to divorce the world of the family almost entirely from the world of work is further illustrated in the experience of a suburban pastor who had a regular practice of calling on his men at their work. He had occasion from time to time to check their work addresses with their wives before calling. To his amazement, many wives did not even know the location of their husbands' jobs. They knew the general line of work, but they had scarcely any notion of where that work was carried on.[45]

The introverted insulation of the family within its idolatrous little confine of privatism and "togetherness," in separation from the husband's daily work, is matched only by its insulation from public issues of moment. The remarks of the Presbyterian researchers on this point deserve quoting: "Countless hours of analysis, dissection of interview protocols, and subsequent reflection upon the many revelations of these middle-class Protestant parents left us with an impression that is sobering for the church: family life is discussed as if it were isolated from the broad currents of society and world events. It is disconcerting for official Protestantism with its world-wide mission and awareness of the complexity of our social life to notice that the typical parent insulates his private family life from the political and economic trends which affect his life so deeply."[46] It is interesting to note that major public issues of the day were seldom part of a suburban interview; the exceptions were the churches where a strong adult education program existed, and in which socially relevant preaching was reported.

The program of Christian family life education in the local church therefore cannot be merely family-centered, in the narrow sense of being concerned only with mutual ministry within the circle of family relationships abstracted from the wider social context in which the family exists. The problem of tensions which are created at work and which are expressed at home must be honestly faced, together with the impact of the value systems of business life upon family values. The impact of international tensions, national issues, and other matters of controversy and aspects of rapid social change upon the family also must be included if family life education is to avoid the pitfall of merely reinforcing the family's proneness to an idolatrous and escapist privatism.

The concern of the people of the church for the strengthening of family life is in itself a valid protest against the depersonalizing tendencies of modern mass society. It is an affirmation of the preeminent worth of persons and their interrelationships. However, the program of family life education in the church must guard against implicitly encouraging its people to regard the family as merely a refuge, a shelter of personal intimacy from an impersonal world. Instead, its orientation should be such as to encourage people to view their homelife as a place for nurturing the humane values and the concern for persons that are so desperately needed today, not only within the home, but also within those wider structures of society where the members of the family also have Christian responsibilities to fulfill. The lay ministry of the members of a family to one another must never be seen as exhausting the meaning of lay ministry. It must be seen as a training ground, an incubator for those personal qualities that are also needed in ministries in civic, political, and economic life.

Chapter VII

Starting Other Vocational Concern Groups

ONE OF THE BEST WAYS for a church to avoid conveying the impression that lay ministry is confined to family life is to provide one or more vocational groupings of a different order. The mere existence of a specialized professional group, or a commercial or industrial group, bears eloquent testimony to a broader conception of lay ministry, even though quite obviously only a very small minority of a congregation can be involved in groups that are sufficiently specialized by vocations so as to be most directly relevant.

As church leaders seek to determine what particular types of vocational groupings are feasible in a given parish, it is most important that they have a thorough picture of the general occupational distribution of the membership. The membership records of many churches do not even list their people's business addresses, nor give any clear information about the work they do. In order to achieve any intelligent long-range strategy for training the laity for their occupational ministries in the world, a church needs to determine both where they are and what they are doing in the world before it does anything else. In connection with almost any kind of parish-wide visitation program, but with especial appropriateness when connected with stewardship visitation, a church-wide census should be taken to determine the location and nature of every member's daily work, and any professional and community organizations he may be involved in as well, for these too are arenas for the exercise of his Christian stewardship. Besides the evident usefulness of this information for educational planning, the very process of conducting the survey to obtain the information has educational value, for it communicates to members of the church the fact that the church regards their secular involvements as an intrinsic part of their total stewardship response. Such a census "teaches" them that the church is interested not only in their financial support and their contributions of time and ability to the institutional needs of the church, but that it also is interested in and affirms their responsible work for community betterment, and even beyond the residential community, their occupational duties as well.

In determining which vocational groups ought to be formed, and in what order, laymen in the various service or helping professions, such as medicine, teaching, social work, and perhaps also those in commerce or industry who are in primarily interpersonal work such as sales, personnel, and supervisory positions, ought to be given some priority of consideration, for a number of reasons. For one thing, the nature of their work is so obviously a matter of direct and tangible service to their fellowmen, or at least it is so clearly a matter of personal relations and communications in contrast with primary relatedness to things, that these lines of work can probably be more immediately and totally perceived as Christian vocations than can occupations in which the service factor and the interpersonal element are more obscured. Next to Christian family life education, concern groups centering around these types of work are probably the easiest contexts in which to sharpen self-awareness of Christian ministry in one's work.

Furthermore, the professional Christian educator who acts as resource person is less far out of his element within the context of such groups than he probably would be in others centering around more impersonal issues, such as questions of Christian responsibility in highly technical types of decision-making. Another advantage in working with such occupational categories is that in convening a group, representatives from a number of such person-centered occupations can be combined around some common denominator of human relations such as a concern for improving communication with superiors and subordinates, helping authoritarian people, handling intergroup conflict, and the like. Finally, this advantage in itself contains two others: it helps to diffuse the pastoral ministry among the laity, making them aware of the various subgroups both at work and elsewhere that constitute the "congregations" within which they may exercise pastoral care, and it gives them helpful insights for this ministry. Actually, of course, laymen themselves can in large measure give each other these insights as they share their own professional knowledge and experience with each other. The religious professional's training and experience in pastoral psychology is only a part, and in some instances a minor part, of the insights into effective ways of helping people that constitute the indigenous resources available to the group. Union shop stewards, department managers, principals, and others often can bring a rich range of perspectives in human relations to one another.

In considering what group or groups might be gathered, the various professions or other vocational specialties do not constitute the only common ground to be considered. The fact that a considerable number of people in a congregation may all work for the same corporation may in itself be a very significant common denominator, even though the specific nature of their work for that corporation may be widely varied. The mere fact of being a "G.M. man" or a "G.E. man," and the need to consider one's real identity and Christian responsibility within such an industrial "family," constitutes an important common concern.

Once a church's educational policy-making body has decided on some particular occupational category for the possible formation of a vocational group, the next task is that of enlistment for participation. Sometimes a simple announcement of intention to form a group may be all that is initially needed to bring to light at least a nucleus of interested persons. In other cases it may be necessary or advisable to extend the invitation in person to a handful of selected individuals, especially when circumstances would seem to dictate a fairly detailed explanation. But whichever method is used, the first step should be to assemble an inner nucleus around which the larger group may be formed, before the total group is recruited or convened. There are a number of reasons for this. For one thing, it would be rather presumptuous for a church's committee on Christian education to select the reading material and determine the place and time and frequency of meeting for a vocational group without prior consultation with at least some of its potential members to determine some of the salient problems and interests of concern to them.

Furthermore, as we shall see, there are strong reasons for involving people from other parishes and even from other faiths in vocational groups. Without prior consultation and careful planning with a nuclear subgroup to ensure the invitation of co-workers who may be intimate associates but who are not members of the sponsoring church, experience has shown that the group is not likely to be ecumenical in composition, to its considerable detriment in many cases. And in the case of a concern group involving workers in one particular plant, it is obvious that the matter of simple physical access to the plant for any outsiders involved, and permission and provision for meeting there, can only be arranged from the inside by some layman. Finally, a personal invitation from another person in the same plant or profession to participate in a group is more meaningful than a mere announcement through parish channels of one-way communication. An invitation coming from another person in the same plant or profession who is already himself committed to the proposed concern group, and who can answer some of the inevitable questions about it, is more meaningful still.

The nuclear subgroup, serving as a steering committee, should determine what stimulus material, if any, should be obtained and read by the group, and what general topics should be considered. It would probably be wise to print this "curriculum," or group agenda, as an intrinsic part of the initial invitation and of each individual meeting announcement. Men in the world of work seldom meet without an agenda, without a fairly specific discussion task, and the amount of anxiety and impatience or even downright hostility that may be engendered by an unbusinesslike lack of explicit structure possibly would more than offset whatever advantages there might be in having a less structured group atmosphere. After all, the curricular agenda is democratically arrived at through the deliberations of the steering committee, and can be altered in accordance with the feedback that may be either volunteered or solicited from other members of the group. It can and probably will be modified at meetings of the entire group or at periodic evaluative get-togethers of the steering committee. The satisfying clarity of delimited discussion objectives that comes from a crisply worded topical agenda commends itself to people immersed in the thought world of modern business; and in many industrial and commercial group situations that necessitate a quite brief meeting time, such as during a short lunch period, the discipline of a task-oriented agenda structure, which in other learning contexts might appear stilted and formal and arbitrary, is a virtual necessity.

Inasmuch as modern commercial and industrial life conditions men to regard the discussion process as a tool for accomplishing specific tasks, as a means for reaching specific goals, it is also probably wise for the invitation from the steering committee to state a specific number of meetings for the proposed group, in harmony and consistency with the statement of specific discussion goals. People are more likely to commit themselves to the discipline of regular attendance and any outside readings of stimulus material if it is known to be for a fixed period of time. By common consent the scope of the discussions can be expanded or the number of meetings devoted to a given topic increased at or before the initially determined cutoff date.

It is also incumbent upon the nuclear steering committee to determine the time and place of meeting. In his study guide for North American ecumenical discussions on "The Missionary Structure of the Congregation," Colin W. Williams, of the National Council of Churches' Central Department of Evangelism, has stated the issue simply and clearly: "If the gathered Church trains the laity for their ministries in the scattered world of secular institutions, it would seem logical that the gathering itself should be at places which are appropriate for training the laity for their scattered life."[47] To say the same thing another way, the adult classrooms in even the most perfectly designed Christian education wing in suburbia may be far less conducive to the kind of adult Christian learning we are talking about here than the quite unholy atmosphere of a noisy, crowded company lunchroom or business-district cafeteria. There is a psychological immediacy to discussions on the meaning of work in the midst of the work environment that is lacking in the leisure-oriented environment of the residential area. It must be recognized, of course, that many vocational categories, such as physicians, salesmen, and teachers, by the very nature of their work are geographically dispersed so that it is usually rather difficult for them to assemble as a group in their work environment. Meetings after hours in homes, or in the education wing of the church, may be necessary for groups of such people; but the first strategic preference should be to place the meeting in the center of working hours, even though there is no geographical center for their kind of work. Vocational groups meeting after hours operate under a certain psychological handicap as compared with noon-hour meetings, which are more *in medias res* with regard to the work environment.

Considerable ingenuity can be employed in arranging both the time and the place of meeting. An example of imaginative adaptation is given in the "Seminar on Wheels" conducted by the First Congregational Church of Chappaqua, New York. Faced with the fact that the many businessmen in the congregation who worked in New York City were widely scattered throughout the city, the minister of education convened a New York Central carload of them for small group discussions from one end of the car to the other during the ninety-minute run from Chappaqua for eight Monday mornings.[48] More recently this idea has been copied in other parts of the country with good results. Perhaps more important than copying the details would be the emulation of the spirit of creative improvisation it reveals.

As was indicated earlier, there are a number of cogent reasons for seeking to include people from other parishes and even other denominations in vocational concern groups. Ecumenical discussions conducted by the Department on the Laity of the World Council of Churches over the years have revealed a strong theological consensus concerning the nature of the ministry of the laity, a consensus almost approaching unanimity when compared with discussions on other questions of faith and order. Consequently, an ecumenically composed group created for the purpose of training the laity for their ministry can assume a wide area of essential theological agreement concerning its central aim, with little fear of treading on any church's doctrinal toes in inviting some of its laymen into such an enterprise. A far more significant argument for an ecumenical group is the fact that the world of work itself, by its very nature, confronts the church as an ecumenical situation. For the most part, functional and friendship relations within the occupational community usually bear little correlation with denominational identification. This is not to say that little parts of the "scattered church" should not be gathered regularly on the basis of their common work life; it is simply an argument for the inclusion of at least a few co-workers who are not members of the convening church but who share the concerns of the group. Professional associations and business enterprises of all kinds will turn a far more sympathetic ear toward requests for access and meeting facilities that are made in an ecumenical spirit than those which request special treatment exclusively for the scattered sheep of one local flock. Furthermore, the establishment of truly ecumenical groups under the initiative of one local church clearly provides the most logical and convenient basis for expansion if and when other churches begin to follow suit in convening groups. Indeed, an ecumenically composed group constitutes a standing invitation and challenge to other churches to do just that. Any purely denominational type of arrangement, developed according to its inner logic, leads by relentlessly imaginative extension to the horrific and scandalous picture of Methodist dentists and Lutheran machinists and Presbyterian salesmen meeting all around a community.

I know from experience that a group must be explicitly and avowedly ecumenical from its inception. This was not done with an industrial study group I convened, and despite all subsequent efforts, it never became truly ecumenical. We were able to attract a couple of men from other congregations of the same denomination, but we never broke the stereotype of denominational identification that became attached to this experimental group project.

In starting a group, it may be necessary in certain situations for the religious professional to assume the role of discussion leader. This is particularly likely to be a necessary expedient in the case of vocational groups in which the workers involved have had relatively limited formal education, such as lower-rank clerical workers or hourly rated production-line workers. In such cases, it may be impossible even after a considerable number of meetings to find a person with sufficient poise and self-confidence and verbal facility to take over this function. However, this kind of group situation should be the exception to the general principle of lay discussion leadership in essentially lay matters. Ordinarily, a lay chairman is far better equipped to guide the discussion in a direction that is germane to the particular issues and problems of his own occupation than is the religious professional, who is basically an outsider in such a group situation. For similar reasons, the introduction of discussion as well as the leadership of discussion seems to be a role for which a lay person is best suited. When the subject for discussion is introduced by a layman, perhaps through the presentation of a case study or a statement presenting his personal position on an issue, the subject is opened in lay language and lay thought forms, and the underlying questions are addressed to the group in a way that is likely to be far more meaningful than a clergyman's opening presentation is likely to be.

As an outsider, an alien visitor to the occupational milieu represented in the group, the optimal contribution the religious professional can make will be as a theological resource person: as one who listens with the perceptiveness of his informed theological perspective, occasionally making comments and answering questions or perhaps raising them as a catalytic agent in the discussion. He simply cannot make this contribution as fully and as effectively if he is trying to fulfill both this role of resource person and the discussion leadership role. If it seems necessary for him to try to juggle both functions when a group is just beginning to meet, every effort should be made as part of the group's own responsibility for itself to remove the mantle of leadership from his shoulders as soon as possible. Freed from the leadership role, from the necessity of attending to every word that is spoken and from the immediate directing of the discussion along the line of the agreed-on agenda, he can concentrate his attention on evaluating the overall functioning of the group for subsequent feedback to the lay leader after the meeting, and listening and absorbing the general atmosphere and movement of the discussion so that he can see how he may best make his own special contribution to the group process.

When the clergyman or other religious professional serving as resource person does make his theologically oriented contribution to the group, he must resist every temptation to pontificate, to short-circuit and preempt that laborious but essential process whereby laymen move from the insights given by general Christian affirmations to their specific vocational applications. The working out of the specific applications to particular work situations of Christian teachings such as those concerning interpersonal relations, ethics, or the meaning of human creativity, is uniquely the work of the laity. They alone possess an existential knowledge of the complex details of their situation, and therefore they alone can carry out the inductive process of applying generalized Christian insights in a way that is not irrelevant or superficial. Furthermore, unless they are the ones who carry out this process, no Christian learning worthy of the name takes place.

The fact that this work of correlation is essentially the work of the laity brings into focus still another argument for lay leadership in the group. The experience of sharing in or participating under lay leadership can lead most naturally and with a minimum of discontinuity to the continuation of a vocational concern group on its own after an initial period of resource assistance during which a religious professional has regularly been present. Such group experience might also smoothly pave the way to the creation of what Bishop Wickham calls "lay projects": vocational groups meeting perhaps during lunch breaks, not only convened but also completely conducted by laymen from the very start, often as outgrowths of their experience in an original group carried on with clerical guidance and assistance. A good example of spontaneous lay initiative in forming such a group comes from the experience of Robert Maynard, a general supervisor in the Test and Development Laboratory of the Cadillac Motor Car Engineering Division in Detroit. Mr. Maynard familiarized himself with the philosophy and program of the Detroit Industrial Mission, and then entirely on his own initiative he carefully selected five graduate engineers who he thought would be interested in forming a vocational concern group. To his pleased surprise, each one eagerly accepted his invitation. They decided to meet during the lunch hour for forty-five minutes once a week for an indefinite period of time. Shortly after they started meeting, four other engineers invited themselves into the group after hearing about it. Six denominations were represented among these nine men. Some of Mr. Maynard's observations are especially worth noting:

You might ask at this point, "How can you possibly hold interest and what do you talk about for over twenty-five meetings?" We initially agreed on three general ground rules. First, we wanted to talk about issues involving our work. Second, we wanted to base our discussion on the theological and/or Christian approach to these problems. And third, we wanted our program flexible enough so that we would discuss what we wanted to and when we wanted to rather than stick to a definitely fixed schedule or program. Such subjects as company hiring policies, salary increases, employee recognition, petty thievery, loyalty to the company, relationship of job and family, drive for money and position, security in our jobs, hiring of colored personnel (and, as a result, the whole field of race relations and integration) were discussed. Other subjects included: What is an engineer? What is a professional? What is work? What is the relationship between work demands and individual morality? What is the purpose of life (a real challenge for us!)? Is DIM (Detroit Industrial Mission) a valid organization? What is the relationship between our church and our work? Actually the list of subjects is inexhaustible. DIM provided reference material for some of these subjects but most of the material came out of our own experiences. We came to no precedent-shattering decisions; the value of the group lies in the educational experience of exchanging viewpoints and gleaning the best of many proposals and in the experience of a new and different level of personal relationships for all involved. . . . We know each other better. We actually have a better understanding of our jobs. This is the only opportunity most of us have to discuss these problems with our fellow workers. . . . I also hope that during the coming year we can start a second or third group. Perhaps these next groups would consist of people from different levels and environments, such as technicians, hourly men, clerks, or men from other Cadillac departments. Our experience this past year has been most gratifying. We have all grown a little taller. . . . If only there were thousands of similar experiences! Perhaps you can start a group where you are![49]

This statement is that of a lay missionary with a clear vision of the essential mission of the church, and committed to a relevant mission strategy of stimulating the gathering of spontaneous little "congregations" that are only very indirectly dependent on professional religious leadership. In this particular instance, no Industrial Mission staff member had functioned even initially in the group as a resource person, let alone as a discussion leader. The help extended by religious professionals on the staff had been given *in absentia,* in the form of printed resources recommended to the group. Such a highly indirect form of inspiration and counsel and guidance need not and probably should not be normative, but it illustrates the extent to which lay initiative can often be relied upon for the furtherance of the church's mission to the world of work.

The less paternalism and clerical dominance there is in the initial leadership of the first outposts of vocational mission, the greater the likelihood that these outposts, these initial groups, will develop in the direction of spontaneous missionary expansion and proliferation through lay initiative. Conversely, the more pronounced the degree of clergy leadership and initiative, the more strongly rooted becomes the spurious impression that the mission of the church consists in the extension of ecclesiastical authority into the realm of secular institutions. The emergence of more apostles such as Robert Maynard of Cadillac depends not simply upon the working of the Holy Spirit but also upon the willingness of religious professionals to trust the manifestations of the Spirit among such laity, and to encourage, train, and advise them in the responsible exercise of their spiritual gifts.

The Moralistic Pitfall

In considering what it means to be a lay minister in one's daily work, many people tend to see the issues strictly in moral terms rather than in terms of basic theological self-awareness. It is often assumed that the difference which being a Christian makes is primarily a moral one. A Christian, it is assumed, will go about his daily work in an ethically upright manner. He will be honest, and will avoid scandal, compromise, and intrigue. The viewpoint expressed in J. C. Penney's autobiography, *Fifty Years with the Golden Rule,* is a good illustration of this tendency. Similarly, the study material prepared by The Laymen's Movement for a Christian World is filled with the most platitudinous and general moral advice, presented as the essence of what it means to be a Christian in one's daily work.

This moralistic line of approach fails to take cognizance of the fact that there is nothing uniquely Christian about being honest or ethically upright in one's work. Christians have no monopoly on the ethical virtues. Many workers are honorable, conscientious, kindly, and thoughtful without invoking Christian sanctions for such virtues. Furthermore, the moralistic tendency to regard Christian vocation as a mandate to conduct a daily job differently as a Christian from the way it is conducted by the non-Christian places the burden of emphasis upon what *men* do to make a difference. All efforts to define and express the Christian calling of every man in terms of moral achievements, however high and noble, betray the fundamental theological orientation of the Reformation itself, especially its insistence that men are justified by faith rather than by their works. According to this doctrine, men are uniquely Christian not because of any special ethical attainments but by responding in penitent gratitude to the grace of God made known in Jesus Christ. While the Christian faith contains no less an impulse to high moral conduct than any other live option of belief, it is far more than exhortation to noble living. It is *good news* rather than good advice. It centers around a message of pardon and healing for men who have come to realize how far they fall from the aspirations they cherish.

Thus the distinctive difference in a Christian's sense of vocation lies on the religious level of an inward relationship to a God of mercy revealed in Jesus Christ. This means that Christian vocation involves the living of life consciously under a sense of judgment and of grace. The judgment is not an abstract or moralistic sense of guilt, but a sober realization that the necessary work of this world is carried on by morally imperfect means, and that the tension between high ethical idealism and practical necessity is resolved at least in part by faith in God's redeeming love. A Chicago banker in the experimental Bankers Occupational Ethics Group convened by Victor Obenhaus, of Chicago Theological Seminary, for the National Council of Churches evidently had been led by this group experience to a highly personal appropriation of this truth of the Christian gospel. The banker remarked in one meeting that "in the face of the problems I have to solve and the delicate decisions I have to make it is essential that I stand forgiven for my failures to fulfill what I know the Christian standard requires of me."[50] Vocational groups should inculcate an awareness of the fact that in a sinful world one's ministry can never be without sin, one's service can never be rendered without compromises that can only be covered by the divine mercy.

This is not to say that vocational groups should not discuss questions of morality in business or the professions. It simply means that all such discussion should be maintained within the context of an adequate understanding of the meaning of grace. Without a theological self-awareness of standing under grace, the members of such a group may superficially seek to justify themselves to themselves or to one another, or perhaps the moralistic tone of the discussion will deepen their feeling that their faith has nothing truly vital to say to their moral dilemmas.

With an adequate understanding of judgment and grace, a vocational group will not ask what is the uniquely Christian thing to do, because it realizes that no moral action is uniquely Christian. Its ethical concern will be motivated by the gratitude of men who know themselves to be forgiven, justified sinners. It need have no other motivation or angle, such as an attempt to pave the way for verbal evangelizing. The New Testament itself recognizes that not all Christians have been gifted for verbal witness, that the spiritual gifts of preaching and teaching are not universally bestowed. Love alone is the one common manifestation of the Holy Spirit. Therefore the witness of the laity in their work does not necessarily imply twisting the lunchroom discussion away from the pennant race to talk about religion. It does imply a loving concern for one's brother as a person, but this may imply affirming him as a person far more by how one listens to him than by what one says to him. Christian concern and service need have no ulterior purpose. They may and probably will help to create situations in which verbal witness becomes possible, but that is their effect and not their immediate purpose. As men consider together the kinds of witness they can make, it is well for them to be helped to realize that Christian love is self-authenticating, and serves as unto Christ, whatever its evangelistic results may prove to be.

Furthermore, Christian love has as one of its manifestations the task of loving service through socially useful acts of human creation. The report of the study section on the laity at the Evanston meeting of the World Council of Churches indicates how an excessively personalistic conception of witness obscures the importance of work itself as part of the Christian's witness:

> Certain inherited false views of work are still in some places effective in dividing the Church from the working world. There is a tendency in some sections of church life to be interested in man only as a soul to be saved without regard to his physical, mental and social welfare. Work is accordingly viewed only as a field for evangelism, a sphere of opportunity for personal witness. While, of course, the Christian layman will miss no suitable occasion for bearing his testimony to the truth, he will regard his job as itself a matter in which he may directly serve his Lord. He will bear witness not only with his lips but by the quality of his workmanship; he will do his work as "unto his Master in heaven." A right understanding of the doctrine of Creation will remind him that God has given to man an awesome capacity to change the face of nature by his work; the wonderful achievements of man in his work must neither be ignored nor regarded as manifestations of his sinful pride.[51]

The foregoing observations serve to underline the fact that the attainment of some modicum of theological self-awareness of man's God-given place in the world of work is the necessary starting point for preparation for lay ministry. The laity do not need primarily to be exhorted to "do" something, to achieve something. What is vitally needed today is to help them understand who they are: the people of God in his world, cocreators with him, and involved in the world as its servants without being slaves to its standards. A theological self-consciousness of *being* is the necessary prelude and key to *acting*.

Consequently, it is of first importance in the life of a vocational group to begin on a note of affirmation: to affirm the importance and meaning of the occupation represented, and all its positive potential for the enrichment and fulfillment of human life. The initial group experience in particular should be such that it will tend to confirm people in the holy significance of their creative responsibilities as creatures made in the image of their Creator and therefore called to be cocreators with him, thereby strengthening basic Christian motivations for the responsible exercise of their occupational power as the servant church in the world. Of course, people do not initially expect this. They expect the church, particularly its professional leaders, to judge what they do rather than to affirm what they are. Therefore one of the first things that comes into their minds when they hear of a vocational group is that this group doubtless will be primarily concerned with occupational ethics, that primarily they are assembling to be judged (or, more hopefully, to sit in self-righteous judgment on "those others" in management or labor or government or among one's competitors, or any other outgroup that may serve as a convenient scapegoat). Consequently, they will assemble with a self-defensive frame of mind that needs to be allayed at the outset if there is to be any openness for new learning; and it cannot be allayed without positive affirmation of the value of their daily work as such.

This affirmation need not and should not be naïvely uncritical; that could amount to the spurious sanctification of bourgeois virtues, the canonization of exertion and efficiency and productivity as such, and perhaps also a rationalization for an economically and politically irresponsible quietism. Still, without the affirmative note being sounded from the outset, it is less than likely that anything else will be heard, and the group may never move out into broader theological issues connected with modern work beyond the strictly ethical issues. The general tone of the group discussion might then become indistinguishable from the fatuous and superficial moralism of the worst kind of Sunday school class. The note of affirmation may be sounded in either implicitly or explicitly theological statements concerning the meaning of work that are incorporated into the convening invitation or in some of the opening sessions. It may also be sounded by how men are listened to perhaps even better than by how they are addressed, by the sheer fact of genuine interest on the part of the professional religious leader in the work itself.

Robert C. Batchelder, of the Detroit Industrial Mission staff, notes the affirmative value of the church's interest, expressed through the listening ministry of one of its professional representatives, in his evaluation of a vocational group of men in the construction industry with whom he had been meeting:

> In addition it must be said from the standpoint of the church that it was good and of some importance that the church showed an interest in these men and their work—that it took seriously what is of great seriousness to them. Apart from

whether the church was able to contribute anything specific in the way of insight or practical guidance, the very fact that it was involved in such a series of discussions was probably of value in implying that what happens in a man's work is of importance to God and in providing support and encouragement to those struggling to improve the practices of the industry.[52]

Questions concerning occupational ethics need to be discussed, as they were in this group, and the word of God's judgment needs to be mediated to men in the midst of their moral dilemmas and in the face of their evasive rationalizing; but this element of judgment belongs within a broader supportive context of theological affirmation in the discussion. Men and women need to be helped to see that God is not concerned merely with the individual and collective morality of people's work lives, but also with such matters as their motivations and satisfactions and vexations in their work, its relation to their homelife and their political activity, the nature and utility of the product or service rendered, the effect of the communications network and the operative decision-making channels on persons, and other wide concerns transcending the merely ethical.

Exposing Myths and Stereotypes

The wider context within which judgment should be mediated is the total work situation itself, and the basic attitudes and frames of reference which men both bring to that situation and also derive from it. Divine judgment is concerned, not only with wrong ethical policies and actions, but also with wrong attitudes and perceptions, those erroneous or half-true shibboleths, stereotypes, and myths which so largely dominate men's thinking like some form of demon-possession. God desires not only that men do justly; he also desires truth in the inward being, and therefore group discussions that expose some of the mythology and folklore of management or labor or any other vocation as containing illusions or falsehoods serve God's purposes in the world as surely as do discussions that are more narrowly centered on occupational ethics. To expose the falsity of some blatantly inaccurate but popular generalization within a group of labor or management people can have a very liberating and redemptively significant effect.

It should be obvious that to the extent possible the prophetic act of exposing such falsity in any given group should be performed by lay people themselves. Since they already expect the clergy to be passing judgment upon them, they are pretty well inured by their self-defensiveness against the clergy's judgmental onslaughts, so that the prophetic observation coming from the clergyman is likely to be easily blunted or deflected with yet another generalization or a shifting of the center of conversation. The religious professional wears the prophetic mantle at still another disadvantage in this situation because of his relative ignorance of the specifics of the vocational milieu. The note of clarifying judgment that brings men to the truth about themselves and their world is heard most distinctly when it is spoken without an alien accent, when it is spoken by one of the people.

The clergyman or other professional religious worker who may be serving as resource person to the group can, however, prompt and precipitate the moment of perceived judgment by the stimulus material and observations he presents or the questions he raises. For example, he may point to some inconsistency in the dialogue, such as the common one in which a group will agree that "sound ethics is good business" and in the next breath will be equally agreed that "if a person tried to follow Christian ideals rigorously in this work, he'd starve to death." Another common inconsistency that may be pointed to and probed is the fact that many business people feel that they have to say that making a profit is their first motive, whereas other motives such as the desire for creativity or status or a sense of social worth may appear regnant in their conversation in the group.

In addition to the thoughtful calling of attention to inconsistencies between statements made within the group, another means of mediating a note of judgment through creative challenge is to point to inconsistencies between statements made in the group and opposing viewpoints voiced by others outside the group, perhaps in the form of speeches or articles or other reading matter covered either by the group as a whole or contributed by any one member of it. Through this kind of confrontation, hackneyed old shibboleths and myths concerning such notions as economic individualism, the primacy of purely economic motivation in human work, unconditional optimism concerning upward mobility through honest effort, or the rationality of "enlightened" self-interest can be demythologized in the sense that group members can be led to perceive such statements for what they are in reality.

An example of the effective use of the method of confrontation through the introduction of an utterly new consideration is given by Harvey Cox, of the American Baptist Convention's Division of Evangelism, in his report of an experimental group of insurance executives convened to discuss their Christian witness in their occupational life. The central function and responsibility these men exercised was the making of investment decisions for the portfolios of their respective companies. However, the general current of their discussion flowed narrowly along the one channel of their personal relationships with other management personnel in their companies. They had fallen into the all-too-familiar trap of conceiving of the relevance of Christian conviction only with regard to interpersonal relationships, utterly failing to see its relevance for the relationship of persons to *things,* i.e., in this case securities portfolios. Thus these men were skirting the issue of the major function of their occupation, which was to make creative and highly responsible decisions between various possible investments. It simply did not occur to them that their responsibility as executives deciding on investments was the major focus of their Christian ministry as workers. They claimed that such decisions were "purely economic," by which they meant that they were made without any value references to their Christian commitment. Cox indicates how the stimulus of a broader Christian concern was successfully introduced at this point by the Commentator (Cox's term for the clerical resource person):

> Because the leader team had made thorough-going preparation, the Commentator was able to point out to them their limited and closely circumscribed view of the relevance of Christian faith to life. Here it became evident that the executives had a picture in their minds of the typical insurance policy holder which understood him also as an "economic man." They had never examined their assumption that the holder of an insurance policy may be interested in other things than the highest possible capital return on his investment. He might be interested, for instance, in having some of his funds invested in endeavors which contribute to the health or cultural welfare of individuals. The session ended with the insurance executives expressing gratitude to the Commentator for having helped them to enlarge their view of how the Christian faith saves them from narrow and mechanical views of their constituency. If it is really true that man does not live by bread alone, perhaps the typical view of the investment counselor of his client as an economic man can be qualified and corrected by a more realistic conception.[53]

While a shift in the discussion from personal interrelations, narrowly conceived, to questions of policy-making apparently was appropriate and timely in this particular group situation, this does not imply that human relationships should be a merely tangential concern for a Christian vocational group. Since the experience of reconciliation is God's intention for his world, group discussions that deal, let us say, with man's inveterate tendency toward scapegoating and stereotyping of those individuals and groups above, below, or alongside him in the world can be of great redemptive significance. Furthermore, questions of policy-making and questions of human relations are by no means mutually exclusive. They must often be considered together, especially inasmuch as policy-making in modern society is so rarely a purely individual undertaking, but is instead a function of the dynamics of group decision. For this reason, vocational responsibility should be considered not only in terms of personal competence and conscientiousness in the performance of an assigned job, whether as an individual or as part of a work team, but also in terms of one's potential or actual causal influence within the society of work. Vocational responsibility requires what Peter Drucker in *The New Society* refers to as "citizenship," self-conscious involvement in the "politics of work," the entire interpersonal process within the community of work whereby decisions of vast importance are arrived at.

To discuss policy-making is, of course, to discuss ethical questions; and although arguments were advanced earlier in this chapter against starting a group out on topics centering on occupational ethics, it is certainly important that a group eventually arrive at this point. The scope of the ethical problem is not to be minimized. A survey of opinion taken among executive readers of the *Harvard Business Review* in 1961 revealed that four out of seven of them believe that their fellow businessmen "would violate a code of ethics whenever they thought they could avoid detection," and four out of five of them affirmed the presence in their particular industry of practices that are generally accepted and that are at the same time unethical.[54] In some of the comments made by the respondents in this survey, and in other voices being raised by laymen in professional and business life, a significant number of requests are being made for relevant ethical guidance from the churches. The guidance they are asking for is neither a matter of highly specific directives at one extreme, nor platitudinous generalities at the other. After all, laymen scarcely need any instruction in determining the difference between fraud and fair play, honesty and dishonesty. On the other hand, they are not inviting the clergy to pass judgment on highly technical and intricate dilemmas whose complexity exceeds the comprehension of any outsider.

Between these two equally irrelevant extremes of ethical guidance there exists what William Temple referred to as "middle axioms": provisional, working definitions of the type of behavior required of Christians at a given time and in given occupational circumstances, located halfway along a continuum between specific problems and abstract ethical generalizations. At one end of such a continuum stand the laymen, with their competence in perceiving the specifics of a given moral problem; at the other end is the religious professional as resource person, with his special competence in the theological groundwork of ethics. The creation of helpful and illuminating "middle axioms" for the occupational group in question is a joint task for the laymen together with the clergyman as they reach out toward each other in dialogue from their opposite ends of this ethical continuum. Quite obviously, a group need not have a clergyman as resource person in order to arrive at such middle axioms; it may have more than enough theological sensitivity and acumen in the persons of at least some of its members. Nevertheless, it is true that the clergyman or other religious professional can contribute much to an informed theological perspective on the basic values and norms that should be incorporated in any truly Christian middle axiom, which in turn will provide illumination for clearly perceiving the ethical issues at stake in any given situation. That is to say, he can make this kind of contribution provided he does not conceive of himself as an all but omniscient moral authority who knows beforehand how the dialogue will or should come out, and what the middle axioms should be.

In dealing with ethical issues, and all other matters of Christian concern, the religious professional must realize that instead of moving deductively from the Christian revelation, the group should first analyze carefully the realities of their particular work—its special demands, satisfactions, problems, and pressures. These realities constitute the question, or questions, to which the Christian gospel can and must address responsible and appropriate answers. It is the task of the religious professional to help laymen to structure and formulate both the questions and the answers. To do this he must listen most carefully to what they are saying about their life in the world. In the words of a statement drafted by the Central Committee of the World Council of Churches concerning the ministry of the laity: "It is becoming clear that one of the main tasks of the Church, when it assembles its scattered members, is to listen to them speaking of their trials and difficulties, hopes and fears, opportunities and needs, and even simply about the facts of life in the world. The assembled Church cannot become a teaching Church until it listens. We urgently need a Church that will teach out of the experience of listening."

Chapter VIII

Toward a Curriculum for Renewal

TO LIVE as a Christian amid the complexities of our modern world is not something that can be done well just by instinct. It has to be learned, and such learning is a combination of a deeper understanding of the gospel together with a thorough use of some of the best descriptive and analytical literature available for the study of man and society. It has often been said that a Christian needs both his Bible and his daily newspaper to guide him in his obedience to Christ in the world. In Christian concern groups, the "newspaper," so to speak, should consist of the raw materials of the job situation, or whatever other area of Christian responsibility a group has agreed to consider.

This concluding chapter is a bibliographical essay suggesting primarily some sources of information and insights to serve as the "newspaper," and secondarily some resources that seek to cast an explicitly Biblical light on these subjects. It is hoped that these suggested resources may prove helpful in building or at least initiating a curriculum for lay training within various types of concern groups. Many of the titles recommended here have been used profitably by groups in my church, and most of them have proved helpful to actual groups known to me at least indirectly from reliable evaluations, if not from my direct involvement. Some of these materials perhaps could be obtained and distributed to those people who will be serving as a small steering committee preparatory to the original convening of the concern group in its entirety. The reading and evaluation of these resources by members of the steering committee would help them to identify and verbalize real problems and issues for discussion, and would guide them toward choices of reading material for the entire group that would be of direct relevance to these identified concerns. The suggestions made here are far from exhaustive, but at least they provide a point of departure for further exploration on the part of the concern group's steering committee and resource person. They can and should be supplemented with articles from current periodicals and new pamphlets as these come to the attention of people involved in the groups.

General Concern for Lay Ministry

In some local church situations it may appear advisable to convene a quite unspecialized concern group, or even a series of such groups, preliminary to any convening by specialized function in the world. Such general groups are, of course, severely limited in their ability to deal with the highly variegated specifics of Christian responsibility in the world, but they can provide a significant leavening influence that prepares the way for involvement in functionally aligned groupings at a later time.

A good text for a general concern group is the study pamphlet *Salty Christians* (The Seabury Press, Inc., 1963), by Hans-Ruedi Weber, Associate Director of the Ecumenical Institute of the World Council of Churches, and prior to that the Executive Secretary of the World Council's Department on the Laity. This pamphlet is based on a handbook for lay training which Weber wrote for the East Asian Christian Conference and personally used in lay training courses all over the world. It has a study guide, prepared by the Department of Christian Education of the Protestant Episcopal Church, containing excellent questions and case studies for discussion. A special virtue of this pamphlet is that both its text and discussion guide explicitly point beyond themselves to the need for more specialized forms of lay training to accord with the laity's specialized forms of ministry in the world.

Another helpful general work of greater length is *The Ministry of the Laity: A Biblical Exposition* (The Westminster Press, 1962), by Francis O. Ayres, of Parishfield, an ecumenical lay training center near Detroit. Ayres has done a good job of translating some of the major insights of such seminal thinkers on the subject as Hendrik Kraemer, Jacques Ellul, and Dietrich Bonhoeffer into language and images far more easily comprehensible for the average layman than the writings of these famous mentors themselves tend to be.

Family Life and the Feminine Role

In recent years the denominations and interdenominational agencies have been producing such a wealth of materials for Christian family life education, at least when compared with the paucity of materials available on other areas of lay ministry, that little needs to be suggested here. However, three paperbacks are worthy of special mention: Reuel Howe's *The Creative Years* (The Seabury Press, Inc., 1958) and *Herein Is Love* (Judson Press, 1961), and Gibson Winter's *Love and Conflict* (Doubleday Dolphin Book, 1961). Among other commendable qualities, these books are noteworthy because they push beyond parental responsibility to include also a consideration of the responsibility of husbands and wives to one another and the scope of their respective roles, and *The Creative Years* and *Love and Conflict* go even farther in relating issues of family life to the public realm of politics, community life, and daily work. *Love and Conflict* is also worthy of recommendation for women's concern groups on the whole issue of the feminine role. It is especially helpful in suggesting a meaningful delineation of the scope (and limitations) of the woman's role in rearing children, and the formative influence she is uniquely able to exert in shaping the uses of leisure and in creating a viable fabric of community within the residential neighborhood.

Betty Friedan's *The Feminine Mystique* (W. W. Norton & Company, Inc., 1963, and Dell paperback, 1964), a very angry book, also has been popular with great numbers of women. It gives an essentially despairing answer to the question of meaning in the homemaker role, insisting that the urge for creativity and a sense of personal satisfaction can be fully satisfied only through a career outside the home. However, the eloquent force of its negativity makes it a useful point of departure for discussions of some of the central frustrations and threats to Christian meaning that homemakers face.

The Problem of Leisure

Discussions on the role of leisure in family life will be enriched by the use of either Sebastian de Grazia's *Of Time, Work, and Leisure* (Doubleday Anchor Book, 1963) or Robert Lee's *Religion and Leisure in America* (Abingdon Press, 1964). Both books are the products not merely of their authors' creative intuitions but also of special group research projects upon which they build, projects conducted by the Twentieth Century Fund and the National Council of Churches, respectively. De Grazia's book would help clarify the semantics of discussion by helping to delineate the important distinctions between "work time," "time off" from work, "free time," and "leisure" in the classical sense, and by qualifying frequently exaggerated estimates of the increased scope of free time and leisure opportunity in our technological era. The book should be read by discussion leaders and resource persons, but its very considerable length and scholarly historical detail, together with its Platonic-Aristotelian rather than Christian presuppositions concerning the significance and modes of leisure, do not particularly commend it for study by an entire group, unless the group is characterized by a rather high level of cultural sophistication. An entire group that wanted to explore the issue of leisure more deeply than is possible using articles from periodicals, even though more and more of them are appearing as leisure is increasingly recognized as a crucial contemporary problem, would be well advised to avail themselves of Robert Lee's book. It is the first book to attempt to develop and articulate a Christian theology of leisure and an attendant Christian ethic of value criteria to guide Christians in their leisure choices, and it succeeds admirably on both counts.

Helping Professions

People in the "service" professions such as medicine and law and teaching, in administrative or supervisory positions in industry, in positions of community leadership, or those who regardless of their official roles are concerned with becoming more effective means of grace and "agents of reconciliation" in their relationships with other people, can profit from a study of Reuel Howe's *Herein Is Love* in this context also. This book presents a helpful exposition of the Biblical doctrine of love in terms of its relevance to psychological realities in all manner of personal relationships. Paul Tournier's *The Meaning of Persons* (Harper & Row, Publishers, Inc., 1957) leans more heavily on some of the insights of dynamic psychiatry and their relationship to Christian doctrine as seen by a deeply concerned psychiatrist. An effective curriculum can be constructed employing either of these works, together with carefully prepared and screened case studies illustrative of the possible application of some of the insights both of them contain.

A concern group consisting of members of the medical profession might consider Joseph Fletcher's *Morals and Medicine* (Beacon Press, Inc., paperback, 1960), supplemented with additional insights from Willard L. Sperry's *The Ethical Basis of Medical Practice* (Harper & Row, Publishers, Inc., 1950). Another commendable title, James T. Stephens' *The Christian as a Doctor* (Association Press, 1960), also concerns itself with questions of medical ethics, but within the wider context of the total meaning of Christian vocation for physicians. It is one of a series of books dealing with specific jobs and professions as Christian callings, under the able editorship of Edward Leroy Long, Jr. Each of these books has been written by a man with personal experience in the field about which he writes. The series seeks to help close the gap between generalized Christian affirmations about Christian vocation and the actual realities of particular kinds of daily work. If a group of physicians should identify the relationship between science and religion as a significant concern for them, they might profitably study physicist-theologian Ian G. Barbour's *Christianity and the Scientist* (Association Press, 1960) from the same series. And for members of the legal profession, lawyer-Bishop James A. Pike has written *Beyond the Law: The Religious and Ethical*

Meaning of the Lawyer's Vocation (Doubleday & Company, Inc., 1963). This small but thoughtful book develops a conception of the lawyer as more than an expert pursuing a highly technical calling, one that urges him to go beyond the law in giving ethical as well as legal counsel, and in other ways participating actively in the formulation of social policy as a "public man" rather than a mere legal technician.

Christian Political Responsibility

The body of literature dealing with various social questions is so vast and so quickly dated that any listing would be highly arbitrary and of questionable value. However, two volumes dealing with the basic Christian rationale for political involvement, together with some practical observations and guidance, that have proved illuminating for many study groups are William Lee Miller's *The Protestant in Politics*, Layman's Theological Library (The Westminster Press, 1958), and William Muehl's *Mixing Religion and Politics* (Association Press Reflection Book, 1958). Miller's book is directed primarily to Christians already active in political affairs. William Muehl, a layman writing for laymen, writes with great practical helpfulness for the relative neophyte who has been steering cautiously clear of direct participation in a political party.

Commerce and Industry

An important source of material for discussion in industrial and commercial vocational groups is to be found in the various periodicals read by union and management. Such materials are filled with assumptions of usually unexamined theological significance. For example, the literature of the unions conveys the general assumption that work is hellish and meaningless, that the boredom of it should not be alleviated through job rotation because of seniority problems, and that the main mission of the union movement is merely to make this hell more financially rewarding. It seems to assume that the possibility of finding intrinsic satisfactions in industrial work is of no concern to the union, that the extrinsic satisfaction of having a larger and more secure slice of the economic pie, together with pleasant and comfortable working conditions, pretty well delimits the extent of the union's legitimate concern with the work situation itself.

Similarly, business and technological literature often conveys the assumption that by means of the scientific method all the really important questions of life can be answered if given sufficient time and money. Questions beyond the reach of scientific investigation seem to be regarded as either unimportant or meaningless, and it is implied that by means of scientific technology the important problems of human society can all be solved. Furthermore, it is often assumed in this literature that economic efficiency is the ultimate measure of social value. Assumptions such as these, expressed in the literature of both labor and management, provide a fruitful point of contact between the Christian gospel and secular ideologies of work. Even a study of house organs, the publications of particular companies for their employees, can be a significant line of approach. Within them a company displays a company point of view, a company way of doing things, a company tradition. Companies have their own interests, their own loyalties, their own ethos and atmosphere, their own set of rules and values. A discussion based on company publications is one of the best ways of bringing some of these aspects of the community of work under thoughtful scrutiny.

An inexpensive yet excellent way in which to listen to what the statesmen of the labor movement are saying would be to subscribe to *The American Federationist*, the official monthly magazine of the AFL-CIO. Their point of view often finds expression also in the Sidney Hillman Reprint Series, which consists of reprints of speeches, articles, and broadcasts on such various subjects as civil liberties, race relations, social welfare, economic security, and international relations. Information concerning quantities may be obtained from the Sidney Hillman Foundation.

As an excellent way to grasp management's point of view, to listen in on some of the most serious and soul-searching levels of dialogue in the business world, and to discover the chief problems and issues of work as business leaders identify them, the *Harvard Business Review* commends itself for a place in the curriculum. Over the years many important issues have been covered in their different aspects and from various points of view in a series of articles, such as the Human Relations Series, the Philosophy of Business Series, and the Religion and Business Series, which have been reprinted and bound together and are made available by the Reprint Service, *Harvard Business Review.* In addition to these series reprints, copies of all individual articles that appear in any current or previous issue are also available.

A number of thoughtful articles that appeared in the *Harvard Business Review* between 1949 and 1959 have been selected and edited by Edward C. Bursk and published as *Business and Religion: A New Depth Dimension in Management*, by Harper & Brothers in 1959. Another interesting anthology including articles from the *Review* and other usable material is the paperback *Living My Religion on My Job*, published by The Layman's Movement for a Christian World, Wainwright House, Rye, New

York. It includes "How Ethical Are Businessmen?", the report of a survey of seventeen hundred *Harvard Business Review readers;* "Can the Businessman Apply Christianity?", an excellent article relating the Christian doctrines of God, creation, sin, and vocation to realities in management situations; speeches by the deans of Harvard Divinity School and Harvard Business School, excerpts from the writings of Cameron P. Hall, Alexander Miller, and even Martin Buber, to mention but a few. This fine anthology is unfortunately encased in a discussion guide and utilization plan which is generally moralistic and trivial, evading basic questions of meaning and direction in work and the ultimate purposes of increased productivity, and geared to the uppermost echelons of management. However, the articles can be used independently of the accompanying guide and suggestions for use.

In 1950, J. H. Oldham wrote the monograph *Work in Modern Society* for the Study Department of the World Council of Churches. Now reissued in paperback (John Knox Press, 1961), it constitutes a helpful statement of crucial issues for modern industrial life such as incentives and satisfaction in industry, the meaning of leisure and its relation to work, and an outlining of what the Christian view of man and of his work has to say to these issues. Robert Calhoun's *God and the Day's Work* (Association Press Reflection Book, 1957) is an old but helpful treatise on the relevance of the doctrine of creation and man's vocation as cocreator to the perception of ultimate meaning in industrial enterprise. Whereas these works by Oldham and Calhoun are chiefly appropriate for those directly engaged in industrial production, either Alexander Miller's *The Christian Faith and My Job* (Association Press Reflection Book, 1959) or Harold L. Johnson's *The Christian as a Businessman* (Association Press, 1964) would be useful as a theological primer on the Christian potential in other walks of business life as well as manufacturing.

Major issues confronting our industrial civilization are examined from a strongly humanitarian and ethically sensitive viewpoint in the series of occasional papers, reports, conversations, and other pamphlet material published by The Fund for the Republic's Center for the Study of Democratic Institutions. Its publications are the fruit of continuing studies of the economic order, the trade union, the political process, the communications industries, the churches, the impact of science and technology, the role of law, and the evolving American character, written by men of nationally recognized prominence. Also worthy of mention, especially for industrial groups, is the series of occasional papers being printed in pamphlet form by the Detroit Industrial Mission. These include statements of the philosophy of industrial mission, reports of vocational groups, essays on the secular relevance of Christian doctrines, and similar items of interest.

Agriculture

Since I have no experience whatever with concern groups of agricultural workers, I am indebted to C. A. Pepper, Director of Town and Country Work for the American Baptist Home Mission Societies, for resource suggestions in this area. Suggested publications of the National Council of Churches include: *Keeping Ethically Alert Amid Rapid Rural Change,* a pamphlet by Shirley Greene which highlights ethical issues in rural life today; a 1958 National Council statement on *Ethical Goals for Agricultural Policy* (pamphlet); *Town and Country Churches and Family Farming* (booklet, with accompanying study guide pamphlet), a summary of factual data by the National Council's Department of Town and Country Church regarding farm tenure and family farm situations in the United States, and their relationships to family and community life; and Rockwell Smith's paperback *People, Land and Churches* (Friendship Press, 1959), which examines the total mission of the church in the rural community. A filmstrip, *Who Is a Christian Farmer?*, based on the actual discussions in an Illinois concern group, raises basic issues confronting the Christian farmer in his daily work and relationships (produced by the United Church of Christ). A thirty-two minute color movie, *Shadow of the Land*, deals with the special problems created by corporation farming in its effects on families, persons, and the work of the church (also produced by the United Church of Christ).

It is hoped that what these listings may lack in comprehensiveness is compensated for by the fact that most of them have been tested and found usable in specific group situations. As the chapter title suggests, this bibliographical essay does not in itself constitute a full-orbed curriculum for lay training, but only a cautiously and tentatively proposed step or two in that direction. Every group must participate in the designing of its own curriculum. No other person or group of persons possesses the omniscience necessary to do this for them. Informal conversations with those participating in the group, or at least among a representative steering committee, is the necessary first step by which the real problems and issues are identified so that a relevant curriculum may begin to be constructed. When this process is followed, materials for study are less likely to be ends in themselves, abstract and impersonal obstacles to dialogue which hold people off from one another at arm's length. Instead, they serve as precipitants and stimulants that open up the central areas of concern at the beginning of discussion, and they also serve to press people on beyond the immediate and obvious to new levels of awareness and commitment.

Notes

1. Roy W. Fairchild and John Charles Wynn, *Families in the Church: A Protestant Survey* (Association Press, 1961), p. 213.

2. Gerhard Lenski, *The Religious Factor: A Sociologist's Inquiry* (Doubleday & Company, Inc., 1961), p. 30.

3. Fairchild and Wynn, *op. cit.*, pp. 174–175.

4. *Ibid.*, p. 175.

5. Herman G. Steumpfle, "Public Relations Executives," *On-the-Job Ethics,* ed. by Cameron P. Hall (National Council of Churches, 1963), p. 110.

6. Georgia Harkness, *The Church and Its Laity* (Abingdon Press, 1962), pp. 15–16.

7. Robert A. Raines, *New Life in the Church* (Harper & Row, Publishers, Inc., 1961), pp. 103–124.

8. Lenski, *op. cit.*, p. 108.

9. E. R. Wickham, *Church and People in an Industrial Society* (Lutterworth Press, London, 1957), p. 230.

10. Arnold B. Come, *Agents of Reconciliation,* Revised and Enlarged Edition (The Westminster Press, 1964), pp. 74–85.

11. Lenski, *op. cit.*, pp. 109–111.

12. Reuel Howe, "Theological Education After Ordination," *Making the Ministry Relevant,* ed. by Hans Hofmann (Charles Scribner's Sons, 1960), p. 159.

13. Hendrik Kraemer, *A Theology of the Laity* (The Westminster Press, 1959), p. 41.

14. John R. Fry, *A Hard Look at Adult Christian Education* (The Westminster Press, 1961), pp. 136–137.

15. Gibson Winter, *The Suburban Captivity of the Churches* (Doubleday & Company, Inc., 1961), p. 156.

16. Gibson Winter, *The New Creation as Metropolis* (The Macmillan Company, 1963), p. 127.

17. *Ibid.*, p. 67.

18. Gibson Winter, "The New Christendom in the Metropolis," *Christianity and Crisis,* Vol. XXII, No. 20 (November 26, 1962), p. 210.

19. Wickham, *op. cit.*, pp. 244–245.

20. Gordon Cosby, "Not Renewal, but Reformation," *Renewal,* III/3 (April, 1963), p. 4.

21. Margaret Frakes, *Bridges to Understanding* (Muhlenberg Press, 1960), pp. 62–63.

22. Klaus von Bismarck, "The Laity: The Church in the World," *Laity,* Vol. 13 (February, 1962), p. 7.

23. Kraemer, *op. cit.*, p. 102.

24. Abbé Michonneau, *Revolution in a City Parish* (Blackfriars Publications, 1949), pp. 13, 16.

25. Kraemer, *op. cit.*, p. 179.

26. Leo R. Ward, *Catholic Life U.S.A.: Contemporary Lay Movements* (B. Herder Book Company, 1959), pp. 54–56.

27. *Ibid.*, pp. 46–50.

28. *Ibid.*, pp. 51–52.

29. George MacLeod, *We Shall Re-build* (Kirkridge Press, 1945), pp. 11–13.

30. Kraemer, *op. cit.*, p. 159.

31. George W. Webber, "EHPP: Emerging Issues," *Union Seminary Quarterly Review,* Vol. XIV (May, 1959), p. 14.

32. Ernest W. Southcott, *The Parish Comes Alive* (Morehouse-Gorham Co., Inc., 1956), p. 139.

33. Wade H. Boggs, Jr., *All Ye Who Labor* (John Knox Press, 1962), pp. 148–149.

34. The Bishop's Company (Drama-in-the-Church, Inc.), an itinerating repertory company, specializes in contemporary plays of theological significance that are adaptable to chancel performances, with the simplest of costumes and props, and a handful of players. The players are most willing to take part in discussions with the audience following a performance. The guaranteed minimum required is modest. Information regarding bookings can be obtained by writing The Bishop's Company, Box 424, Santa Barbara, California.

35. Films Incorporated (4420 Oakton Street, Skokie, Ill.), a subsidiary of Encyclopaedia Britannica Films, not only rents 16mm. films of significant movies of even quite recent years but also provides intelligent and thorough discussion guides written with considerable sensitivity and theological depth. In addition to Films Incorporated, the following film libraries may be contacted for catalogs and other information:

Association Films, Inc., 561 Hillgrove Avenue, La Grange, Ill.

Brandon Films, Inc., 200 W. 57th St., New York, N.Y.

Cinema Guild, 10 Fiske Place, Mt. Vernon, N.Y.

Contemporary Films, Inc., 267 W. 25th St., New York, N.Y.

Fellowship of Reconciliation, Box 271, Nyack, N.Y.

United World Films, Inc., 542 S. Dearborn St., Chicago, Ill.

World Wide Pictures, P.O. Box 1055, Sherman Oaks, Calif.

36. Daniel Jenkins, *Beyond Religion* (The Westminster Press, 1962), pp. 116–117.

37. Wickham, *op. cit.*, p. 225.

38. John A. T. Robinson, *On Being the Church in the World* (The Westminster Press, 1960), p. 85.

39. *Ibid.*, p. 23.

40. Franklin H. Littell, *The German Phoenix* (Doubleday & Company, Inc., 1960), p. 123.

41. Wickham, *op. cit.*, p. 251.

42. Fairchild and Wynn, *op. cit.*, p. 136.

43. Boggs, *op. cit.*, p. 16.

44. Fairchild and Wynn, *op. cit.*, p. 193.

45. Gibson Winter, *Love and Conflict* (Doubleday & Company, Inc., 1961), p. 34.

46. Fairchild and Wynn, *op cit.*, p. 158.

47. Colin W. Williams, *Where in the World* (National Council of Churches, 1963), p. 82.

48. Edwin D. McLane, *The 7:05 and the Church Alive* (Prentice-Hall, Inc., 1963), pp. 26–33.

49. "Field Report: Cadillac Engineers," *Life and Work,* Vol. 6, No. 1 (Fall, 1963), pp. 3–4.

50. *On-the-Job Ethics*, p. 20.

51. The Report of Section VI, "The Laity: The Christian in His Vocation," *The Evanston Report,* ed. by W. A. Visser 't Hooft (Harper & Brothers, 1955), pp. 163–164.

52. Robert C. Batchelder, "Men Who Build: Some Human Problems in the Construction Industry," Occasional Paper No. 5 (Detroit Industrial Mission), p. 21.

53. Harvey Cox, *Manual for Church in World Witness* (American Baptist Home Mission Society, 1960), pp. 48–49.

54. *Living My Religion on My Job* (The Layman's Movement for a Christian World, 1962), pp. 46, 50.